# EMOTIONAL INTELLIGENCE GUIDE

## 4 Manuscripts in 1 Book

# DAVID CLARK

This book set includes:

Book 1) Emotional Intelligence: A 21- Day Step by Step Guide to Mastering Social Skills, Improve Your Relationships, and Boost Your EQ

Book 2) Cognitive Behavioral Therapy: 30 Highly Effective Tips and Tricks for Rewiring Your Brain and Overcoming Anxiety, Depression & Phobias

Book 3) Mindfulness: How to Create Inner Peace, Happiness, and Declutter Your Mind

Book 4) Empath: The Essential Guide to Understanding and Embracing Your Gift While Using Meditation to Empower Yourself

# Table of Contents

**Emotional Intelligence** ......................................................................1

    Introduction ...........................................................................3

    Chapter 1: Understanding Emotional Intelligence....................................9

    Chapter 2: Identifying Your Own Emotions.............................................19

    Chapter 3: Managing Your Emotions .....................................................33

    Chapter 4: Managing People's Emotions ...............................................47

    Chapter 5: Secrets of Building Healthy Social Relationships.................63

    Conclusion ............................................................................75

**Cognitive Behavioral Therapy**...........................................................77

    Introduction .........................................................................79

    Chapter 1: All About CBT ......................................................81

    Chapter 2: Basic CBT Toolbox..............................................93

    Chapter 3: Exposure Therapy ...............................................99

    Chapter 4: Dealing with Cognitive Dissonance.....................105

    Chapter 5: Dealing with Persistent Negative Thoughts ........110

    Chapter 6: CBT Techniques for Dealing with Anxiety...........115

    Chapter 7: CBT Techniques for Dealing with Anger.............120

    Chapter 8: CBT Techniques for Breaking Bad Habits ..........125

    Conclusion ..........................................................................129

**Mindfulness**.....................................................................................131

    Introduction .........................................................................133

    Chapter 1: Creating Inner Peace ..........................................135

    Chapter 2: Creating Happiness .............................................140

    Chapter 3: Decluttering One's Mind .....................................146

    Chapter 4: Being More Aware ...............................................152

Chapter 5: Eliminating Stress...................................................154

Chapter 6: Being in the Present Moment...............................158

Chapter 7: Benefits of Mindfulness ........................................161

Chapter 8: How to Incorporate Mindfulness into Everyday Tasks .....164

Conclusion...................................................................................166

**Empath**....................................................................................**169**

Introduction...............................................................................171

Chapter 1: The Traits and Price of High Empathy ..............173

Chapter 2: Understanding the Gift........................................182

Chapter 3: Are you an Empath? ..............................................191

Chapter 4: Shielding yourself from Harm .............................197

Chapter 5: Stop Taking on the Burdens of Others ...............207

Chapter 6: The Empath's Purpose...........................................209

Chapter 7: Meditation and why it helps................................215

Chapter 8: The Seven Chakras ................................................218

Chapter 9: Your Guide to Healing Meditation......................231

Conclusion...................................................................................239

# EMOTIONAL INTELLIGENCE

*A 21- Day Step by Step Guide to Mastering Social Skills – Improve Your Relationships, and Boost Your EQ*

# INTRODUCTION

*"If your emotional abilities aren't in hand, if you don't have self-awareness, if you are not able to manage your distressing emotions, if you can't have empathy and have effective relationships, then no matter how smart you are, you are not going to get very far."*

-Daniel Goleman

Social skill is a general term that covers multiple aspects of your social interaction and communication with other people. Used in the context of emotional intelligence, social skills are used to manage and influence the emotions of others effectively. This skill set is not something akin to manipulation, but it is as basic as understanding a person's emotions to guide their behavior in a manner that is suitable for maintaining harmonious and productive relationships with others. Consciously or subconsciously, we are intuitive to people's actions and reactions at an emotional level. We are aware of the fact that when we smile at someone, he or she will feel good and return the smile. It breaks the ice and makes us appear friendlier. Smiling makes the other person feel more positive about you.

Social skills are one component or piece of the emotional intelligence puzzle. It originates from a firm grasp on your emotions, followed by the ability to manage it effectively. Next, comes an understanding of other people's emotions and the ability to manage them effectively to fulfill your goal and theirs.

Emotional intelligence and social skills originate from the premise that when you master the art of identifying and managing your own emotions, it is easier to understand and manage the feelings of other people (often referred to as putting yourself in their shoes, or empathy). You begin to understand their emotions by seeing things from their perspective and are therefore in a much better place when it comes to influencing or persuading people.

When you understand how people feel and think, it is easier to tap into those emotions and channel them for influencing people or developing fruitful relationships with them. This is how emotional intelligence can be woven into social skills.

Communication and social skills are vital to emotional intelligence, and vice versa. Their relationship is interdependent and dynamic. It is about developing an ability to listen to someone keenly, understand their thoughts and feelings, and finally being able to persuade them into taking suitable action.

Just consider this scenario to understand how emotional intelligence can impact your social relationships. A co-worker who is not very emotionally intelligent has a heated argument with your boss and goes home immediately afterward.

As soon as he steps into the house, he sees his children playing and making noise and starts yelling at them. The person has acted purely out of his inability to manage his emotions.

Similarly, now think you've just returned home after a heated argument with your boss. When you return home, it is noisy, and your children are making a mess all over the place. You experience the urge to snap but tell yourself that the little children have nothing to do with the argument you've just had with your boss.

They know nothing about what you've been through, and they're just being themselves. You realize that the real cause of your agony is your boss and not the children, who always play in a similar manner. They smile at you and continue playing; you return their smile and go into another room to relax for some time.

What did you do differently than your not so emotionally intelligent co-worker? Rather than acting without an understanding of his emotions, he gave in to his emotional impulses.

You, on the other hand, identified your emotions (thus realizing the anger is misplaced) and learned to control your emotions rather than succumb to them. You put some effort into understanding your emotions and reacted to them in a manner that can be called emotionally intelligence.

Notice how, when there is a rather heated debate or meeting going on, some people will just watch, observe and listen to others carefully when they are unsure of what to say. Even this is a sign of emotional intelligence. When people don't know what to say, and they stay silent without reacting, they are generally processing and identifying other people's emotions through close observation and listening before giving their verdict or pitching in with their two cents on the matter.

Some people are of the opinion that emotional intelligence cannot be learned. It is an inherent knack that we either possess or don't possess. However, psychologists and emotional intelligence experts have turned this school of thought on its head by claiming that emotional and social intelligence is, in fact, something we become mindful of only during the course of our life.

We all come into this world as selfish beings who cry for attention, food, and cleanliness. If we didn't learn emotional intelligence, all of us would only be screaming or crying for attention and other needs that require fulfillment (something people who lack emotional intelligence are adept at).

Empathy is the main component of emotional intelligence. When you learn to empathize with people and establish connections, they are more likely to listen to you and do what you want them to. Your ability to understand and manage emotions such as anger, joy, anxiety, sadness, shame, love, optimism, fear, and more, to a larger extent, determines how successful you'll be not just in your social life but also in your personal and professional life.

Think of yourself as a hiring manager. You have two similarly qualified, experienced, and professionally capable candidates. They possess more or less similar expertise on the subject matter and are applying for the same senior position. However, one of them displays a better ability to understand and manage other people's emotions, thus making him a perceptive and influential leader.

Who do you think has better chances of being successful and contributing to the organization as a productive leader? Obviously, someone with more evolved emotional intelligence. It has been established through countless studies that employees with high emotional intelligence can lead teams more effectively, adapt to change, and make for better team players. As technology evolves, forming connections with people becomes all the more relevant and important.

Is it possible to develop emotional intelligence in 21 days? Yes and no! First, nothing works on its own. So, when someone asks me, "Does this program really work?" I turn back and say, "It depends on whether you are willing to make it work!" Nothing works on its own unless you make it work. If you are willing to make a 21-day plan work, you will see results. If you don't make it work, results will elude you. It is as simple as that.

# CHAPTER ONE:

# UNDERSTANDING
# EMOTIONAL INTELLIGENCE

*"When our emotional health is in a bad state, so is our level of self-esteem. We have to slow down and deal with what is troubling us so that we can enjoy the simple joy of being happy and at peace with ourselves."*

-Jess C. Scott

## What is emotional intelligence?

Emotional intelligence is the ability or knack to perceive (or identify), manage, and evaluate emotions within one's self and other people. It is not just about being in possession of this knowledge but also knowing how to use this information suitably.

It was in 1990 that two Yale University psychologists coined the term "emotional intelligence" that has found wide acceptance today. Later, psychologist Daniel Goleman popularized the term through his emotional intelligence book.

Emotional intelligence, even in the context of developing social skills, begins by learning to tune in to your feelings and emotions.

## What are the characteristics of emotional intelligence?

In his book, psychologist Daniel Goleman offered a broad framework of five essential characteristics that comprise emotional intelligence.

## Self-Awareness

People who possess high emotional intelligence are generally self-aware. They have a firm grip on identifying and managing their emotions, which makes it near impossible for their feelings and emotions to overpower them. They rule their emotions instead of the other way around. They are more confident and self-assured because they have complete trust in their intuition, and they don't allow their feelings to spiral out of control. Emotionally intelligent people can take an unbiased and objective assessment of their positives and negatives, and they are more than willing to work on their weaknesses. Self-awareness, according to several psychologists, is the key component of being emotionally intelligent.

## Managing emotions, or self-regulation

This characteristic of emotional intelligence is the ability to manage emotions and inherent emotional impulses. Being aware of your emotions is only half the battle won. Managing, controlling, or regulating these emotions is equally important. For instance, people who are emotionally intelligent can identify when they experience emotions such as anger, envy, etc. However, they will not let these emotions get the better of them. These people will find a way to manage destructive emotions without making impulsive, hasty decisions in the face of these seemingly powerful emotions. They use knowledge of their emotions in the best way possible to manage or control their feelings and behavior effectively.

Self-regulation can be practiced in many ways, including being aware of your values, holding yourself completely accountable for your actions, and practicing being composed and calm even under the most stressful situations.

## Motivation

Motivation is another important characteristic of emotional intelligence. People who are self-motivated work towards their objectives consistently, while setting high standards for themselves and others. Get into the habit of re-examining why you do what you do. If you are engaged in a business or job, why are you doing it? Stay hopeful and look for a more positive mindset. Each time you are faced with a seemingly adverse situation, look for a valuable lesson in it. Find different ways to keep yourself motivated and charged.

## Empathy

It isn't an understatement to say that empathy is the backbone of emotional intelligence. The essence of emotional intelligence is to be able to identify not just your feelings or emotions but also those of other people around you. Empathy is the ability to place yourself in the other person's shoes and understand things from his or her perspective.

If you are in a position of leadership, few qualities are as important as empathy to gain loyalty and respect from your followers or team members. Empathetic leaders have a knack for developing people, challenging people who act in an unjust manner, offer constructive or positive feedback, and actively listen to people.

There are plenty of ways to increase empathy, and these include:

## Placing yourself in another person's shoes

It is easy to support your own perspective or belief. However, try to think of a situation from a point of view that is opposed to yours to better understand what the other person is thinking or feeling. Look at any situation from diverse perspectives.

## Respond to people's feelings rather than ignoring them

Let us take an example here to drive home the point more effectively. You order your secretary to work late today to finish scheduling important meetings and making travel plans. He or she agrees with you (obviously, they won't say no), but you have sensed a slight disappointment in their voice or body language. It is clear that they don't appreciate staying back late for work. As a person in a position of authority, you can either ignore it (they will still do their work), or address their feelings. Ensure you mention to the employee that you are aware how he or she doesn't like staying late and that you really appreciate them going out of the way to help meet the organization's goals. Throw in a line about how you yourself are stressed about working late. You are addressing his or her feelings and letting them know that you really appreciate it or want to find a solution for it. Next time, compensate for it in some other way or find a solution such as allowing him or her to come late one day when there isn't much work to be done.

## Social skills

Social skills and emotional intelligence are often interwoven. People who are emotionally intelligent can identify and manage other people's feelings more effectively. They are efficient at managing change and diplomatically resolving disagreements. There are several ways to build social skills, including learning conflict resolution, negotiation, enhancing your communication skills, learning to read people's verbal and non-verbal skills, and acquiring the skill of praising others.

Yes, these are essentially the five pillars of emotional intelligence and described by Daniel Goleman. Let us look at another example of how people with high and low emotional intelligence will react to the same situation in different ways.

Person A has been awarded a rather coveted and prestigious project at work. He or she is under tremendous pressure to put in their best and complete the project successfully. This is a rather stressful and challenging situation, and though he or she should be happy about bagging such a huge project, it is natural for him or her to be nervous, too. A majority of the people will feel the pressure and be stressed out as a result since that is the first emotional impulse. We are primarily wired for reacting to situations rather than thinking things through. However, now another person (Person B) can utilize stress for channelizing his or her energies and using the opportunity to shine in the eyes of higher management. He or she will initially feel overwhelmed by the responsibility, but this feeling will soon melt into seeing the situation as an opportunity and a willingness to take the challenge. They will get a grip on themselves and start working towards accomplishing their objective. Emotionally intelligent people are balanced in the truest sense. They know how to convert negative or seemingly stressful emotions into positive results.

## What Is the Difference Between Intelligence Quotient and Emotional Quotient?

A lot of times, people ask the basic difference between emotional quotient and intelligent quotient explained in a way that's easy to understand. Simply put, while intelligence quotient is a measure of a person's cognitive abilities, emotional quotient is an indicator of his or her emotional intelligence.

The technical skills that you have learned and acquired over a period of time contribute to your cognitive abilities or emotional intelligence. Intelligence quotient determines how technically competent you are when it comes to fulfilling a professional role, and how successful you will be in performing that role.

However, we live in a world of changing social dynamics. Technical skills and cognitive abilities are not the only factors that influence a person's success. People must also master the art of controlling one's own emotions and other people's emotions as well as to nurture rewarding social relationships. Unless you live in a rabbit hole and plan to stay there all your life, you will need to interact with people every day.

Let's see how emotional quotient and intelligent quotient differ and how they are relevant to personal and professional success.

Take a scenario where you have been appointed to head a rather prestigious project that your organization has just bagged. Doing this project well could mean a lot of business for the firm. Of course, you will be given a team of proficient and skilled people who will contribute to the project.

Successful completion of the project will involve staying back after work and intensive research. Some people will have to stay back to finish the project on time. Now your technical skills or intelligence quotient will determine how technically fine the project turns out to be.

However, it is your emotional quotient, or emotional intelligence, that will determine how motivated your team stays while performing the project in the face of pressure, stress, and additional work hours. Will you be able to influence and inspire your team to put in extra work to stay on track throughout the project? Will you be able to handle the ego clashes that may arise during the project duration? How will you keep the team focused, productive, effective, and positive to create a desirable result? How will you help them cope with a high-pressure situation? All of this is determined by your emotional intelligence.

Our intelligence quotient is a combination of our inherent intelligence, (mainly hereditary), knowledge, and ability. However, the way we manage people or deal with their emotions is driven by our emotional quotient.

Isn't it simpler to work with people in a way that is beneficial for everyone when you can gain an understanding of their emotions? What are the feelings and emotions that drive people? What triggers people to act in the way they do?

For instance, someone who suffers from low self-esteem and excessive self-criticism may be driven by public appreciation, while someone who is more self-assured may be driven by monetary benefits, accolades, and rewards. When you understand the emotional make-up of a person, along with his or her personality, it is easier to tap into the things that drive them to get the best out of them. It is important to identify the underlying feelings and emotions behind people's actions, and this is possible only when you are emotionally intelligent. This is the basic distinction between intelligence quotient and emotional quotient.

People in public life such as political leaders, advertisers, social media influencers, and social campaigners do nothing but use emotional intelligence to stir public opinion in their favor and persuade or influence people to take their side.

Advertisers are always tapping into emotions related to aspirations, greed, jealousy, and fear to convince their target audience what to buy. Having knowledge of your demographics is an example of one showing their intelligence quotient but knowing how to use the most intrinsic emotions to persuade customers to buy your products or services is nothing but a sign of emotional intelligence. Their promotional messages are filled with visuals and subtle, yet clever, undertones that are designed to play on people's basic emotions.

Another fundamental difference between emotional quotient and intelligence quotient is that while our IQ stays more or less the same throughout our lives, our emotional quotient is evolving. Unlike IQ, it can be developed with consistent training and practice. EQ is a more flexible variant and can be cultivated or evolved throughout your life.

While people with a high IQ are adept at tasks that require complex technical skills and cognitive abilities, they will struggle with social relationships if they aren't high on emotional quotient. They will seldom recognize their own or other people's feelings, which leads to resentment and stressful relationships. These people tend to struggle with social adaptability and internal feelings, thus leading to conflicts.

# CHAPTER TWO:

# IDENTIFYING YOUR OWN EMOTIONS

*"Emotional intelligence is the ability to sense, understand, and effectively apply the power and acumen of emotions as a source of human energy, information, connection, and influence."*

-Robert K. Cooper, PhD

Start the first day by knowing yourself completely. Being self-aware is the cornerstone of emotional intelligence. When you are self-aware, you identify your own emotions and become more mindful of them on a minute to minute basis, thus recognizing the feelings created by these emotions and the ability to manage them in the best possible manner.

People who are self-aware will seldom be overpowered by their emotions. When you know how you think and feel, it is easier to understand your entire emotional framework and stop being a victim of your own destructive emotions. You hold complete control over how you respond to any situation. This leads to greater self-assurance and the ability to form mutually beneficial relationships.

Here's how to develop greater self-awareness:

## Day 1: Journaling

Journaling is a wonderful way to gain deeper insights into one's thoughts, feelings, and emotions at the beginning or end of each day or anytime during the day, actually. It's like taking stock of your emotions the way you would take an inventory of physical products.

Write what exactly you felt when something specific happened during the day, including physiological reactions, sensations (faster heartbeat, sweating, dizziness, etc.), and more.

I personally like to make a list of roles that I actively fulfill on an everyday basis. For instance, parent, partner, co-worker, gym buddy, etc. What are your feelings towards each role at the end of the day?

You may be a very content parent but a frustrated professional. Similarly, you can be a happy spouse but an anxious businessperson. From day one onward, think of each important role and your feelings towards the role. When you identify your own feelings for every role, you get more power in controlling those emotions towards that specific role. It will not just increase your understanding of your feelings towards that role but also put you in control of your own feelings and emotions when it comes to that relationship.

## Day 2: Do a Mental Check-In

Do what pesky yet well-meaning house-keepers and guest services personnel do at hotels. They knock on the door and keep asking you if you need anything. Similarly, you knock on your mental door (without really saying, "Do you need cleaning services or perhaps some tea or coffee?") and tap into how you are feeling at any given point. You can actually do this multiple times a day. Take a complete account of your emotions. Where are those feelings originating from? Why are you feeling the way you are feeling? What physical signs indicate those feelings? Do your feelings and emotions follow in quick succession? Are they accompanied by physical sensations? Are these emotions visible through your body language (expressions, gesture, leg movements, posture)? Are your feelings easily noticed by others? Are your decisions driven by your emotions? Even though it is a near impossible exercise, try to observe your emotions in a neutral and non-judgmental manner.

For instance, if you don't agree with a co-worker about something, try to delve deep into the reasons. What has prompted your disagreement? Are you genuinely in disagreement with the point raised by your co-worker, or is it simply a clash of egos? Are you simply envious of the person or dislike him or her because of some reason that leads to your disagreement with one another?

Professional sportspeople are offered intensive training in emotional intelligence. Yes, a sport is a competition of physical prowess, but the attitude of competitiveness, handling stress, overcoming obstacles, and winning begins in the mind. During crucial events, when an athlete can identify and manage his emotions in the best possible manner, it impacts their performance and chances of winning dramatically. Similarly, their performance is not negatively affected by their feelings and emotions.

When you are fully aware of your feelings and emotions, you know your strengths and weaknesses. These realistic expectations give you greater confidence and leave little room for disappointment. This eventually leads to greater overall social adaptability and competency.

When you gain greater awareness of your own and other people's feelings, you don't become a prisoner of emotions. There is a greater control over your responses, which increases your sense of self-worth.

Labeling your emotions is another fine way to run through your emotional experiences. This helps people in several ways, including recognizing fundamental triggers of specific negative emotions. Whenever you feel the need to identify what causes you to think or act in a certain way, write down the precise emotion of your experience. As much as possible, you must also include what triggered the emotion.

For instance, what makes you angry towards a particular person? Is it something to do with the way they are as a person or your own low self-esteem or self-assuredness? Or is it to do with a bias that has been deeply ingrained into you by society? Be honest and write down what triggers specific destructive emotions in you. Once you recognize triggers, it is easier to manage or respond to those triggers.

Sometimes you may hate a person simply because you believe they have a better life than you, and what you could be experiencing may be nothing more than jealousy pangs.

When you identify the feelings as jealousy, you are in a better position to deal with these potentially damaging emotions. Labeling gives you the right perception to develop a clearer understanding of your emotions. Thus, we can manage our responses or reactions in a more constructive manner.

Also, pay attention to physical clues when it comes to identifying your emotions. By getting into the habit of listening to your body, you will realize that your body can tell you a lot about how your mind is feeling.

Our physical and mental selves are more entwined than we believe. They have a profound impact on each other. When you pick physical signals from the body, you'll get a clue about your emotions too. For instance, if there's a knot in your stomach, or your breathing pace quickens, or the chest feels rigid, you may be stressed or nervous. Sadness makes your limbs slow and heavy, and it takes a lot of effort to walk down even a few steps. Similarly, extreme joy and nervousness increases your heartbeat and gives you butterflies in the stomach.

You are simply identifying your emotions and not judging them. All emotions, whether negative or positive, are valid. Judging our emotions is not recommended because it will unnaturally inhibit the manner in which these emotions are expressed.

Treat each new emotion like a new piece of information linked closely with what is happening inside your mind. You will be at a loss about how to react appropriately without connecting with your inner self. This is exactly why the power to identify and manage your emotions is a type of intelligence which is sometimes believed to be even more important than regular intelligence quotient. Experience both positive and negative emotions and learn from them. Even if you are feeling an intensely negative emotion, it will tell you something about the situation.

I'd go a step further and state or name your emotions. Research in the field of neuroscience and neuro-linguistics suggests that naming your emotions is one of the simplest yet most effective ways to reduce its intensity.

What you are doing is taking the spotlight away from the emotion and thinking about emotions in a cognitive manner. Another trick is to speak about your emotions as a third person. For instance, instead of saying, "I am annoyed," try saying, "John is annoyed." If that appears too weird or freaky, try, "I am undergoing a feeling of annoyance or irritation." It leads to neutralizing intense emotions and acts as a more soothing mechanism.

Treat your emotions as some sort of information or knowledge rather than something that needs to be resolved right away.

Name your compelling emotions and let the emotions last for a few seconds without giving in to the urge of reacting to them. Just feel them for a while without doing anything about it. Allow yourself to feel angry, jealous, frustrated, annoyed and pretty much anything else that you are feeling. The more you try to push out or stop feeling something, the more these feelings will bounce back. According to physiological research, it takes around six seconds for our body to absorb emotion-related chemicals.

## Day 3: Mindfulness

Mindfulness is another brilliant way to gain self-awareness at any given time. While some people recommend setting aside a fixed time for meditation, I'd say you can even practice it during a quick coffee break. Mindfulness is about developing a connection with your deeper, inner self. It is about enhancing your intuition or your ability to tune in to what your inner self is trying to communicate with feelings and emotions. You train yourself to "listen" to your feelings and emotions as they occur in the present without judging them. When a consistent mindfulness practitioner develops the habit of identifying feelings as they originate, he or she gains priceless insight about their emotions, which ultimately helps in resolving several pressing issues.

Mindfulness teaches you to be in the moment and identify emotions as they occur. How to meditate or practice mindfulness?

Nothing fancy. Just sit on a chair or the ground in a comfortable posture. Use support (if required) in the form of pillows. Close your eyes. Start by focusing on your breath. Notice everything from the sensation of the air entering your lungs to the process of exhaling. Clear your mind from all regrets of the past and anticipations of the future. Eliminate all stressful situations from the mind. Your mind should be a blank slate that includes no feelings and emotions. Count from 1-4 each time you inhale, and then four counts again when you exhale. Keep the breath slow and focused. Don't focus your thoughts on what is beyond your control. Rather, focus only on the breath by calming your thoughts. Even if your thoughts wander, bring them gently back to the breath.

Another way is to breathe by counting 1, followed by breathing out at the count of 1. Slow down a bit and now inhale at two counts (1-2) and exhale at two counts. Next, make it even more relaxed and slow it down to 1-3, and eventually 1-4. Repeat in a pattern you are comfortable with.

Observe how your lungs feel when a fresh supply of oxygen reaches them. How does the throat feel when air passes through it? How does your stomach feel?

Mindful meditation helps build tremendous self-awareness. When you meditate, you gain the ability to reflect on your actions without being affected by them. Reflection helps you connect with yourself and developer higher self-awareness. Find a calm, undisturbed corner in your home (or workplace) and devote time to an activity that helps you get in touch with your inner self.

Mindfulness is essentially a Buddhist practice that is great for concentrating all attention on the present.

Daily mindfulness induces a sense of calmness, which is ideal when it comes to recognizing feelings and emotions in an objective manner and manages them more efficiently by gaining a better perspective of the situation.

When you come to appreciate the present, you develop a calmer and more focused mindset that is ideal for making decisions or reacting. You learn to tune in to every sensation and emotion to gather a better perspective on life. When you are tempted to respond, you learn to think through your emotions in an objective manner and get a firm hold over them.

Mindfulness can be practiced in several ways, including mindful eating, driving, or walking. Observe your emotions while going out for a walk all by yourself or while eating a meal alone.

All our emotional experiences also impact us physically at some level though we aren't always aware of it. When we become emotionally tense, our bodies instinctively react on a more primordial level in response to a threat. It's an involuntary chemical reaction where our blood vessels contract, the heart rate increases, and our breathing becomes more rapid.

However, this reaction to stress can be calmed if we reduce the emotional stress quickly. Each time you feel emotionally stressed, take a deep and slow breath. Breathe gradually and deeply. Focus on allowing the air to circulate in and out of the abdomen. Do this for a while, and you'll feel like there is a fresher batch of oxygen entering your body. The chemical reactions in the body will put you in an indisputably better state of mind before you begin interacting with others or face a potentially stressful situation.

Even in social situations, train yourself to pay attention to physiological signs of emotions. There are consistent physical patterns connected with each of the six basic human emotions. Reduced sensations in the limbs can be an indication of intense sadness, or sensations felt in the digestive system can translate into a feeling of utter disgust. Similarly, rage leads to heightened sensations in the upper limb region. Surprise, anxiety, uncertainty, and fear lead to sensations in and around the chest area.

Mindfulness is a purposeful, non-judgmental way to appreciate the present and acknowledge your emotions without attempting to push them away. If you do feel fleeting emotions while practicing mindfulness, simply acknowledge it and move back to the focus of your attention without being overwhelmed by it.

## Day 4: Get Feedback

How do you improve your performance in the workplace? You can do it through your annual appraisal, feedback, or evaluation session with your manager or with the human resources department. Together, you conduct an overview of your annual performance, while identifying strengths and areas for improvement.

Why can't this be applied to your personal or social life? Why not get trusted opinion from family and well-meaning friends? They can offer their candid and unbiased views to help you gain a straightforward perspective on your emotions. Let people know that you are looking for genuine, constructive, and straightforward feedback.

Don't get offended by genuine feedback offered by people. Listen to them without succumbing to the urge of reacting or justifying or rationalizing your acts. People should be comfortable giving you their unbiased opinion. Listen to their views carefully without filtering them. You can ask for honest feedback by saying something such as, "I trust your judgment completely which is why I am seeking an honest and unbiased opinion from you, is that alright?"

I also know someone who has appointed little soldiers within their group to call out their behavior when they are doing something they shouldn't or when there's something they want to change.

For example, if you have the habit of hogging the limelight at all social gatherings and genuinely want to give up the tag of an attention seeker, get someone to call out your behavior gently and personally each time they find you trying to hog the limelight. Let your family member or friend know that they have to discreetly point out the actions you wish to change. The same also applies to a professional set-up. Get your managers or other formal channels to regularly offer you constructive feedback. It helps you tap into your strengths and work upon your weaknesses to boost emotional intelligence and social skills. Get a 360-degree reality check on multiple core competency areas.

Self-awareness is never going to be a brief pursuit. It is a lifelong journey that will keep helping you when it comes to developing greater emotional intelligence and evolved social skills. Though self-awareness is a constant pursuit, the points mentioned above will put you on the right track.

## Day 5: Observe the Connection Between Your Emotions and Actions

What is your reaction to overpowering emotions? What is your gut response to situations faced on a daily basis? The more efficiently you can identify what triggers your behavior, the greater your emotional quotient will turn out to be.

You'll know what you need to change your behavior pattern if you can establish a clear link between your emotions and actions. For example, when you feel embarrassed, uncomfortable, or insecure, you may withdraw from a conversation and go into a shell. Similarly, you may raise your voice each time you are angry or even walk out of a room. Some people start panicking or crying when they are nervous or overwhelmed. Understand the specific behavior that drives your emotion, which will help you wield more control over your actions.

Also, don't forget to celebrate positive emotions. Emotional intelligence is not just about identifying and managing challenging emotions. It is also about the power of celebrating positive emotions to attract even more of them. People who celebrate and experience positive emotions not only enjoy more fulfilling relationships but are also more resilient when it comes to responding to the not so positive emotions or events.

Purposefully do things that add more value to your life or make you happy. Small things like practicing gratitude or being thankful for all that you have, engaging in random acts of kindness, thinking about or visualizing positive experiences, eating healthy, and exercising can go a long way to putting you in a more positive frame of mind while thinking or interacting with others.

# CHAPTER THREE:

# MANAGING YOUR EMOTIONS

*"We define emotional intelligence as the subset of social intelligence that involves the ability to monitor one's own and others' feelings and emotions, to discriminate among them and to use this information to guide one's thinking and actions."*

-Salovey and Mayer

Now that we know how to build greater self-awareness of our feelings and emotions, it is vital to know how to manage them efficiently. Knowing or being aware of your emotions is the first step towards being in control of them, and therefore, building more harmonious relationships. Here are some proven tips for managing your emotions to make the most of any situation:

## Day 6: Acceptance of What Cannot Be Changed

Understand that much as you want to, you can't control or change everything around you. There are many things that are beyond your control. Learn to be more accepting of things that can't be changed. Focus on developing the art of gratitude and learn to count your blessings. At the end of each day, start writing ten new things that you are thankful for. It should be a new list each day.

Stop in your tracks each time you feel the urge to complain or criticize, and instead find something good in the situation. For instance, instead of complaining about waiting at the doctor's or in traffic too long, listen to a motivational podcast or read a book.

Be grateful for how you could squeeze in some time for a productive activity. People who are constantly criticizing and complaining about things around them do not possess very high emotional intelligence and emotional adaptability. Consciously practice staying calm and finding the positives even in the most seemingly negative situation. Change what is possible (and within your control) and learn to accept what cannot be changed.

Also learn to accept responsibility for your feelings, emotion, and behavior. They originate from you, and therefore, you are fully responsible for them. If someone says something to you, and you shout back in rage, you are responsible for it, not the other person. You are not a puppet controlled with strings.

Your actions are solely your responsibility. Knowing your feelings can offer you valuable knowledge about your interaction with others. It will also offer insights about your own requirements and preferences. However, these feelings are never the responsibility of another person. When you begin accepting responsibility for your emotions, feelings, and behavior, it will have a positively huge effect in all areas.

Acceptance of what cannot be changed also includes letting go of the past. Unwanted emotions such as guilt, regret, pain, etc. consume our mental energy and prevent us from staying productive.

Emotionally intelligent people seldom cling to their past and know when it is time to move on. Rather than hanging on to the pain and discomfort, they focus on things that are within their control – the present. Gradually eliminate negative emotions and feelings related to the past that have no relevance to your present. Don't harbor emotions that symbolize shame, regret, guilt, etc. Instead, focus on moving beyond them to lead a more positive, gratifying, and rewarding life. It is easier said than done, but gradually eliminating these negative emotions will pave the way for the mind to be occupied by more constructive and positive emotions.

## Day 7: Practice Neutral Thinking

Most of us tend to think in black and white without practicing the art of neutral or balanced thinking. Change the frequency of your thoughts from negative to positive or neutral. Pinch or whack yourself (physical signal is important) each time you find yourself thinking in extremes.

Challenge the feeling and replace it with more positive thoughts in the absence of clear evidence in support of your negative thoughts.

For example, when you send a text message to a friend or call them and they don't reply, rather than thinking that he or she is avoiding you or doesn't care about you, try to think of something that is more plausible and realistic. A majority of the time things are not as bad as we imagine them.

We tend to think in highly unrealistic and exaggerated terms even in the absence of strong evidence. Instead, think about all the times that the friend answered your call or replied to your messages promptly.

Think about the times he or she has been around for you unconditionally. Try to stack evidence in favor of more positive or neutral thinking every time you find yourself slipping into imagining the worst. Maybe the friend is occupied with something or in a situation where it is tough for him or her to give you attention.

Get into the habit of mentally gathering evidence to oppose negative thoughts, feelings, or emotions about others, and increase your capacity to think positively. This is not to say that you shouldn't think rationally or always put on rose-tinted glasses even in the face of glaring evidence. It just means practicing neutral thinking makes you more emotionally resilient and intelligent. You learn to gain a more holistic perspective of the situation rather than limiting your thinking. This is wonderful from the perspective of managing emotions more effectively.

Negative thinking often leads us into a damaging and vicious cycle of negativity, which is harmful to our emotional development. Every time you nurture a negative thought or emotion without any evidence, you impede your mind's ability to think in a more balanced manner.

Also, get out of the habit of making a mountain of a harmless molehill. Pick your battles carefully, or you'll end up stressed and disappointed with pretty much everything around you that doesn't go your way. Determine if a situation is indeed important enough to invest your precious emotions in it.

Not everything that happens around you deserves your time, energy, emotions, and attention. Avoid blowing up situations when it can be controlled. Impossible as it sounds to some of us, avoid reacting on trivial matters.

How can you change the way you think about something from negative to positive? Let's consider some examples. When you don't feel good about someone's behavior, don't immediately jump to a conclusion. The same situation can be viewed in many different ways. Practice looking at things from a more objective and neutral perspective.

Avoid personalizing everything. As humans, we are all guilty at some point or another of personalizing people's behavior and situations. We tend to take people's actions and reactions personally.

Each time someone doesn't answer his or her call when we call them, we instantly see it as them ignoring us or not being sensitive to our feelings. We seldom consider the possibility that he or she may be extremely preoccupied with something, and hence, view the act in a more objective light. People don't do things to purposefully make us feel miserable about ourselves, as much as we want to believe otherwise.

A majority of people do what they do because of the way they are or how they think, and that hasn't got much to do with us. So stop taking everything personally, and understand that what people do is more a reflection of what they are rather than what you are. The best way to rule out misunderstanding and conflict in relationships is to simply widen your perspective.

Another huge negative thinking pattern is fear of failure or rejection. One of the best ways to combat the fear of rejection is to give yourself multiple options in an important situation. Avoid putting all your eggs in a single basket emotionally. There should ideally be a Plan B, C, and D, too, if A doesn't work out.

For instance, owing to a fear of rejection, instead of saying, "I will be totally heartbroken if I don't get this job," say, "I am applying for four equally amazing roles. If I don't make it in one, there are three more options that I am very well qualified to fulfill." You are killing the fear of rejection from its roots.

Although emotions can impact us negatively or positively, which is why we call them negative emotions or positive emotions, there is no such thing as bad emotions. We often establish a rather hostile relationship with our negative emotions, believing them to be bad or something that should be suppressed.

The idea isn't to suppress your emotions but to manage or control them. Think of your emotions as objective or neutral data that is present to help our existence. It is liberating to get out of the mindset of classifying your emotions as good or bad. Taking control of emotions involves being friends even with the seemingly bad emotions.

Think of it like this, your feelings are not meant to be conquered or discarded. They are meant to be expressed and indulged in an intelligent and imaginative way.

Emotions are nothing but neurohormones that are released in response to our perception of people and events. They are meant to direct us towards taking constructive and productive action with a distinct purpose. For instance, fear sends a message that something is a threat, which urges you to protect yourself against the threat.

## Day 8: Avoid Playing Victim

All of us have fallen prey to the victim syndrome where we imagine that the entire universe is conspiring against us. The victim mindset limits your capacity to think rationally and in an emotionally intelligent manner. We can't control people or circumstances around us all the time. However, we can indeed control our reaction towards these circumstances. Get out of the habit of playing the victim and learn to take control of any situation. Also, learn to accept your limitations and accept mistakes if you want to stop playing the victim and evolve into a more socially adept and emotionally intelligent individual.

Notice if there's a clear pattern in your emotional history. This way you learn not just about your feelings but also about how other people's feelings impact you. When you feel a rather compelling emotion, question yourself if you experience it often.

When was the last time you experienced a similar feeling? What are the feelings that preceded and followed it? When you recognize a pattern, there can be greater control over it. How did you handle the situation when it occurred last time? How would you like to handle it in the future? I'd recommend noting your emotional reactions in a journal so you have records of your emotional reactions and social interactions.

## Day 9: Combine Logic and Emotion While Making Key Decisions or Reacting

Get into the habit of stopping before you feel the urge to react or make a decision and think twice. If you take time before reacting, you give yourself the chance to make a decision that is the best for everyone involved. Even emotionally triggered responses can be handled with quick thinking. For example, if your manager yells at you, and you feel the urge to give it back as good as you got it, refrain from reacting and think for a couple of minutes.

The manager may be under immense stress and pressure to perform and handle several employees or team members like you. It isn't about you personally, but about the situation that is making him or her angry and tensed. This may be a personal issue that is bothering them. Take "time off" from your urge to react, and practice greater empathy to understand the person and situation more objectively before reacting.

In the above example, instead of screaming at your manager, assertively state that you understand the situation is tough for him owing to pressure from higher authorities, but you are also doing the best you can to ensure that things go exactly as planned. Assure him/her that you don't intend to let him or her down.

Stopping and thinking before you react is a great way to build more intelligence and sharpen your social skills. It makes you a good mediator and negotiator while saving any situation from going downhill due to an overkill of unrestrained emotions. I would even say, mentally run through the consequences of different reactions, and then take your next step.

So, just like a film, you quickly play out each scenario in your mind before determining the one that works wonderfully well for everyone involved. So, assuring your manager that you are working to the best of your capacity will probably calm him down. Once he has calmed down, he may speak to you in a more encouraging and neutral manner, thus motivating you even more.

Similarly, if you catch an employee acting in a dishonest or unethical manner, you can handle the situation in multiple ways. Weigh down the pros and cons of sacking the employee. Are you going to lose a talented employee to a one-off indiscretion? Was there something that prompted him or her to act in a manner that they did? You could either sack the person immediately after being triggered by a knee-jerk reaction (and probably lose a skilled employee), or you could weigh the pros and cons of a situation before making a decision. Evaluate every situation objectively before making hasty, impulsive decisions.

Practice determining how to behave before actually reacting to any situation.

One of the best tips that I can offer from personal experience is to respond rather than react. Reacting is a more involuntary, unconscious mechanism which is driven by emotional triggers. We often act in a subconscious manner to express or give vent to our emotions. For instance, when you are irritated because you were interrupted by a person several times while you were preoccupied with something important, the involuntary reaction is snapping at the other person.

However, responding to such a scenario needs a more evolved or matured emotional intelligence. Responding is mindful, conscious, and well-thought. It is a more conscious process that helps you decide how to behave. For instance, in the above scenario, if you are pre-occupied with something important and someone interrupts you several times, instead of snapping, you change the approach. You notice how you are feeling or identify your emotions.

This is followed by determining how you will behave. Now, there are several ways to behave such as snapping at the other person, letting the person know why you don't want to be interrupted at this time, and more. Responding is carefully choosing the most mature response without succumbing to the most involuntary or subconscious behavior.

When you are dealing with particularly difficult people, it helps to be proactive and not reactive. One of the important things to tell yourself is that difficult people behave the way they do because of issues related to themselves.

It has got nothing to do with you. Stay reasonable, logical and considerate, depersonalize other people's behavior, or view it in a more objective light. Come up with different reasonable approaches to resolve the issue without personalizing it or blaming yourself for it.

Considering consequences is an important aspect of asserting yourself or standing up for your position. If articulated assertively, it compels the other person to shift their difficult behavior to compliance and bring about a more positive overall change.

Another pro tip for managing your feelings and emotions is to change the body and mind's sensory input. The old school suggestion of counting up to ten may not always work in a situation where you are feeling particularly tense and reactive. Each time you feel overwhelmed by anger or other negative emotions, give yourself a physical jolt to snap the body and mind out of the feeling or breaking the cycle or pattern of thought. You can slap yourself out of it or quickly do some exercise. Do anything physical, any kind of movement or action that gives a little shock to the body and breaks your regular anger or stress mental pattern.

One of the best ways to handle negative emotions is to funnel them into something productive and valuable. Find ways to divert your mind and convert these negative emotions into something solid, positive, and productive.

# CHAPTER FOUR:

# MANAGING PEOPLE'S EMOTIONS

*"Too often we underestimate the power of a touch, a smile, a kind word, a listening ear, an honest compliment, or the smallest act of caring, all of which have the potential to turn a life around."*

-Leo Buscaglia

Social skills take on several forms. It goes beyond being friendly, chatty, and popular. It is about being an ace collaborator, team player, and negotiator. All these are acquired life skills that can be improved upon if we truly care about building them. It takes plenty of time and perseverance to develop the ability to acquire a greater understanding of people's emotions. It is best to practice when a natural opportunity arises.

Emotional intelligence in the context of social skills involves empathy and negotiating for others' needs along with yours. It can be anything from looking for a common ground with other people, to managing people in a professional environment, to being increasingly positive and persuasive.

## Day 10: Develop Keen Listening Skills

Show interest in what people are speaking about and respond in a sensitive and understanding manner without feeling the need to judge them. Don't let your thoughts wander when they are speaking; ask them questions, offer affirmations, acknowledge what they are saying through verbal and non-verbal gestures. Paraphrase or summarize what they say so they know you are actively listening. When you want to practice greater empathy and social-emotional intelligence, it is important to let people know that you are listening to them. This also leads to greater clarity in the conversation.

Sometimes, all people need is someone to listen to them in a non-judgmental manner without offering solutions or getting into the quick-fix mode. Offer statements that will make them feel like you are listening to them and acknowledging their feelings. Statements such as, "Yes, I can understand how you must be feeling," or, "The way you've handled it is truly remarkable." Statements like these can assure them that you are placing yourself in their shoes and offering encouragement without offering solutions or judging them.

From now on, pay conscious attention to your interaction with people. At the end of each interaction or communication ask yourself these questions:

Did I listen to the person deeply? Was I too preoccupied to actively listen to him or her?

Was my body language changed to match the mannerisms of the person I was communicating with?

Did I rephrase what the other person said or ask him or her questions about what they were saying?

Answering these questions will give you a good idea about whether you were able to actively listen to the person and connect with him or her emotionally.

How do you get a person to talk so he or she listens or speaks more about his or her emotions? Many people complain that it is impossible to get a glimpse of people's feelings or emotions.

A pro tip and quick fix for this is to ask open-ended questions instead of yes or no questions. You are throwing open the door for people to enter and share their emotions. Asking open-ended questions is a good way to keep the conversation flowing and getting them to talk. And when people talk, you get the opportunity to actively listen to them.

## Day 11: Practice Being More Flexible and Agreeable

Uncomfortable as it sounds, not everyone is going to agree with everything you say. Every individual can have their own opinions, views, beliefs, and thoughts while perceiving the same matter; it can be quite different depending on how you see it. Openness, agreeability, and flexibility are the basis for developing higher emotional intelligence when it comes to interacting with other people. You must be firm enough to stick to your opinion while still accepting the other person's right to disagree. Even if you don't subscribe to their views, you must try and understand where they are coming from. A narrow mind is not a sign of high emotional intelligence. An open mind, on the other hand, indicates understanding, acceptance, and reflection. It paves the way for better conflict resolution and negotiation. You acquire the art of handling disagreements in a more self-assured, calm, and open manner.

One of the best ways to develop a more flexible and agreeable mind is to watch or participate in healthy debates on controversial topics. Observe how expert debaters put forth their opinion in a firm yet respectful manner without undermining their opponent. See how the moderator sums up the debate in the end to find an agreeable statement that meets both opinions halfway. Being open and agreeable also opens up more possibilities for you and makes you even more socially aware. While listening to television debates, learn to consider both viewpoints and look for more subtle aspects with greater scrutiny.

Also, a lot of people expect other people to react in a manner that is similar to how they would react in a situation. Not everyone's emotional reaction is going to be similar to yours. Consider why someone reacts differently from you and try to understand things from their perspective without judging it as the wrong way to react just because it is different from your way. For instance, you may feel possessive and jealous about your partner mingling with members of the opposite gender, while he or she may not have such an intense emotional reaction to your socializing with members of the opposite gender. This doesn't immediately infer that they love you or care for you any less. It just means that you both are different people who have been through different circumstances, which may have led to one of you being more possessive than the other.

You may have been in past relationships where your partner has not been faithful to you or you may have grown up in an environment where people were not loyal in their relationships. There may be an inherent sense of insecurity that people tend to leave you after a while or that you are not good enough. There can be issues related to confidence, self-acceptance, and self-esteem. Similarly, your partner may have gone through a different set of circumstances, where he or she has learned to be more trustful, self-assured, and easy-going when it comes to relationships. Therefore, he or she isn't affected by your proximity to members of the opposite gender. Get into the habit of viewing things in a broader light when it comes to people's emotional reactions. When your boss doesn't go ga-ga over a project that you've put your heart and soul into, he or she may not be very expressive, or they may have come to expect the same high standards from you, and it may not be something surprising for them to react in a manner that you expect them to. This is important when it comes to understanding things from the other person's perspective.

There is one hack I like to practice just to hone my ability to be more open and flexible. Take an argument that you have really believed in for a long time. Think of all the arguments that support your stand. Now, just to flip it on its head, take up a position that is completely opposite to what you've always believed in. Think of all the different arguments to solidify the opposite stand you've taken. Consider things from a completely different angle. Then apply this to everyday situations each time you find yourself disagreeing with someone's way of thinking or feeling. For example, if you believe your manager is not being reasonable while denying your leave, think of it from his perspective. Defend the manager's action in your head.

What could his or her reason be? Maybe there's pressure from higher management to meet targets and deadlines. Maybe the company is behind their goals or targets, and everyone has to pitch in for a prestigious upcoming project. Ask yourself questions as if you are the manager, and you'll get into the empathetic mindset. You'll be in a better position to understand and accept their decision rather than oppose it.

Another huge sign of emotional intelligence is the ability to be open to constructive criticism. How does a person react when you offer him or her constructive feedback? This will give you a good idea about an individual's emotional intelligence. People with underdeveloped or low emotional intelligence will get defensive or offer a bunch of excuses to cover up their shortcomings. However, those with more developed and evolved emotional intelligence will seldom resist accepting or acknowledging their flaws and passing the buck for their shortcomings onto others. The easiest thing to do is to succumb to your emotions and take a defensive stand. However, recognizing that these emotions arise and then managing them effectively to take the criticism in a more positive and constructive manner is a sign of high emotional intelligence. People with high emotional intelligence seldom take criticism or feedback personally. They realize that no one is flawless and that feedback is a great way to move another inch closer to perfection. People with high emotional intelligence will dive into their inner selves to figure out what went amiss, and how it can be prevented in the future. Their focus will be on listening to the other person rather than proving your point all the time. Emotionally intelligent people rarely hurl accusations, counter-accusations, argue, or reply back. They will listen keenly and focus on enhancing their skills, rather than obsessing about being right or winning the argument. They are also likely to be more accepting of suggestions and constructive criticism, which helps them accomplish their goals. Developing emotional intelligence is about listening to other people, absorbing information and implementing it.

I know plenty of people low on emotional intelligence who get extremely offended even with constructive criticism. Even a tiny constructive or positive suggestion can leave them seething with anger. To develop greater emotional intelligence, increase your appetite for constructive criticism. Rather than feeling offended, try to understand the lessons you can learn from the situation. I know it is near impossible to feel neutral when you've put everything into a project, only to have it ripped apart by your manager. However, think of how it can help you get even better at what you do. You always face two choices in the face of constructive criticism – one: to feel offended and not accept the fact that there is further room for improvement, and two: to put aside your defensiveness and anger and learn vital lessons from the seemingly negative situation.

## Day 12: Develop Greater Empathy

Empathy is the essence of emotional intelligence for better social skills. Recognize how other people are feeling and thinking, and share their emotions in a manner that you can feel the emotions the way they are experiencing it. Empathy is the ability to put yourself in the other person's shoes and identify their feelings and emotions. You don't simply feel bad for them, but you actually feel what they are feeling and understand what they're going through. There is a greater ability to experience and understand their feelings. Develop greater empathy by actively talking to people and tuning in to what they are saying. If you pay keen attention to what they are saying, it will give you a good understanding of their feelings or emotions. This information can help you take better decisions and boost your emotional intelligence.

To boost empathy, simply place yourself in the other person's position. Think how it is to be in their situation. Actively visualize the experiences they must be going through. What can you do to make it simpler for them? I do this at times. When someone is sharing an intensely emotional experience, ask yourself how you would respond in a similar situation.

Sometimes people won't tell you how they are feeling, yet you want to reach out to them and empathize with them. This is where analyzing people and body language comes into the picture. Read what people leave unsaid through their body language. Be intuitive when it comes to catching the frequency of other people's feelings and emotions.

Observe their facial expressions, gestures, eye movements, posture, etc. while talking. Is the body language in sync with what they are saying? For instance, is someone saying they are not bothered by anything but clearly looking fidgety and preoccupied (fidgeting with their hands, not making eye contact, tapping their feet)? Body language or non-verbal clues can be a clear giveaway when words don't reveal much.

Learn to read between the lines, or what is left unsaid. For example, if you serve someone an elaborate multi-course meal and at the end of it, ask them how it was, and they say, "The dessert was good," you can interpret that in different ways. They may have meant that the dessert deserves a special mention because it was exceptionally good. It can also be a subtle way of saying that nothing stood out except the dessert or that everything else was ordinary. You must learn to listen carefully to what people say but even more carefully to read what they leave unsaid. They often say one thing, while their body language reveals the opposite, more insightful truth. Learn to be more observant and pick up less obvious clues that people use to convey their deepest emotions. These less obvious clues are often missed by the other person, which gives you a definite advantage when it comes to understanding other people's emotions.

If you aren't skilled at interpreting clues, do a fun quiz to understand non-verbal signals.

Sometimes, when you are waiting alone at a coffee shop, airport, or doctor's clinic, utilize your time reading people's non-verbal signals. What background do they most likely come from? Where are they headed? What is their profession? How are they currently feeling? What emotions does the tone of their voice indicate? What does their body language say? Do their words match their body language? This will make you more adept at reading people, including everything they don't express.

Developing greater empathy doesn't mean becoming a part of someone's emotional drama. There is a flipside to empathy, too, when people overdo it and are completely consumed by other people's woes. Being emotionally intelligent and empathetic simply means listening to people, offering advice if required, and extend understanding of their situation. However, it isn't about letting other people's emotions, feelings, and lives impact your own.

Empathy should be extended not just to others but also yourself. Start by showing yourself empathy by trying to comprehend why you feel the way you do. What is it that leads you to think and behave the way you do? You may not find an answer immediately. However, keep observing your emotions, and you'll gradually begin to notice various possibilities about why you feel a particular emotion. For instance, if you are always feeling insecure or distrustful in relationships, it may be because of the negative experiences you've had in previous relationships. The feeling may also have its roots in your childhood when you experienced unfaithfulness in relationships and this left a permanent imprint on the brain. Paying close attention to the source of your feelings and emotions will help you deal with them more effectively.

## Day 13: Understand the Impact You Have on Other People

Alright, so now you are gradually able to understand other people's feelings and emotions, but that's not all if you don't know the effect you have on them. How do you make other people around you feel? In what way does your presence impact them? Do they feel nervous, upset, angry, conscious, happy, positive, etc. when you are around? What happens when people are talking, and you walk into a room?

Observe the way you impact others over a period of time. Do you tend to get upset and pick fights quickly with close friends and family members? Do people tend to be more mindful and careful of what they say when you are around because you are easily hurt? You may have to alter your attitude slightly to enjoy a more positive emotional effect on others. Seek the opinion of trusted friends and well-wishers about where you can improve emotionally. Do you need to be less sensitive and touchy? Do you need to build more emotional resilience?

Another aspect of understanding the impact you have on other people is to be emotionally honest. You can't tell people you are absolutely alright and sulk at the same time. That's not honest communication and doesn't make you come across as emotionally open and honest. Practice being emotionally transparent, so people can analyze or read you more effectively. Learn to be more vocal when you are upset, sad, and happy to enable people to understand you more efficiently. This leads to greater trust and less confusion in relationships. People know exactly where you are coming from when you are emotionally open, which leads to better understanding and more rewarding connections. Your emotions must also have a clear boundary, where you shouldn't cross them and hurt other people.

## Day 14: Aim to End on a Cooperative Note

From today, consciously practice ending all arguments on a cooperative note. Of course, this is easier said than done. Social skills go beyond meeting and interacting with new people and mingling with people who belong to different mindsets and playing games. The most important set of social skills today probably relates to negotiations and conflict resolution. Understand exactly what you want and express it clearly. Also, understand what the other person wants or where he or she is coming from. Always aim to find a middle way rather than making it a battle of emotions or egos. Much of emotional intelligence depends on your ability to resolve potential conflicts and come to a reasonable conclusion.

One of the best ways to resolve conflict is to identify a conflict situation. Before jumping to a conclusion in a volatile situation, take your time. There's no pressure to take an immediate decision, though we often make snap decisions in rage only to regret it later. You have plenty of time before making a decision. Consider various solutions before making a decision. Be empathetic to other people's opinions, but be assertive of your own opinion too.

Whether in social, personal, or business relationships, focus on cooperation. Always aim to end things on a cooperative note. Aim to end things with a positive and assertive note as well. Your co-worker, partner, and friends should be aware that you are working on similar goals as they are even if you have differing or conflicting views. The aim should never be to win arguments. It should be to make it a win-win situation for everyone involved. People who want to win arguments at any cost are often people who possess low emotional intelligence.

Of course, social skills are not just about conflict management. However, it is in conflict management that your emotional skills can be best applied. Arguments or differences are resolved only when one can communicate things clearly, understand the other person's perspective, and arrive at a ground that's acceptable to everyone. This clearly needs plenty of emotional intelligence.

Some people work wonderfully well with others, while isolation brings out the best in some. Collaboration and co-operation lead to shared plans and ideas, and a more productive atmosphere.

Here are some quick pointers for managing people's emotions more effectively:

Consciously practice being kind or being compassionate to others, especially those who are less fortunate than you.

Spend time with real people, talking to them and experiencing their company in person rather than on social media.

Be accepting or open to things happening around you rather than resorting to increased criticism of circumstances or people. Be aware or mindful of all the good that your present is offering you.

Exercise to release feel-good chemicals like dopamine in the brain which puts you in a more positive frame of mind for managing emotions more efficiently.

Challenge negative thinking by considering every possible evidence against it. For instance, if you are tempted to think that a person doesn't care about you, think of every instance where he or she has provided their care and affection beyond measure.

Spend time outdoors to enjoy fresh air and nature. It is known to have a calming effect on your emotions.

Sometimes, something as simple as distracting yourself by reading a book, watching your favorite television show, or watching stand-up comedy videos can help you get a grip on your emotions each time you feel overwhelmed by them.

Take time out to thank people or appreciate them for the wonderful things they do for you. Recount and remember all they have done for you, and thank them for it.

Count your blessings. Rather than focusing on the ills or negatives of your life, notice and be grateful for all the wonderful blessings you've been bestowed with. Trust me, there are way too many than what you actually believe. Everything from your eyesight, to the house you live in, to your family and friends, to your limbs is a blessing that not everyone is fortunate enough to have. Avoid the urge to constantly compare your life with others and complain.

Always play your strengths and focus on doing what you are really good at and enjoy doing.

# CHAPTER FIVE:

# SECRETS OF BUILDING HEALTHY SOCIAL RELATIONSHIPS

*"No one cares how much you know until they know how much you care."*

-Theodore Roosevelt

Yes, when you listen keenly to people, empathize with them, and try to understand things from their perspective, it paves the way for healthier and more rewarding relationships. We must understand that emotional intelligence is not a static skill that we acquire and will last a lifetime. It is a lifelong process and skill that keeps evolving as we navigate various relationships. However, there are a few established tips that will help you sharpen your emotional skills and help you relate to other people more effectively, thus helping you build strong relationships. Here are a few tips for using the power of emotional intelligence to build healthy relationships:

## Day 15: Isolate One Skill

If you are looking to improve emotional intelligence and social skills, rather than trying to be good at everything, isolate one skill that you want to develop at a time. For instance, you may want to work on your listening skills or develop greater empathy. Don't try to work on too many aspects at a time. Identify one component of social-emotional intelligence and observe someone who is particularly good at it. If you know a friend is really good at listening to people and making them feel comfortable, try and observe how they manage their emotions, react, and speak. How does their body language reveal that they are keenly listening to the other person? How do they acknowledge what the other person is saying? What are the usual words they use to make the person feel comfortable? This technique has been suggested by none other than the father of the term "Emotional Intelligence," Daniel Goleman himself.

## Day 16: Open Yourself Up to Establish a Connection

One of the fastest and most surefire ways to build a connection with people is to listen to their experiences with empathy and link it with a similar experience you've undergone. This exchange of similar experiences strikes the right chord in people and makes them open up to you. Don't be afraid to open up a bit and share a similar experience when the other person is sharing theirs. For instance, someone may talk about how painful it has been to grow up in a single parent home. You may be tempted not to share that information about yourself too early on or open up before knowing the person really well, but it can help establish a connection. You can add how you completely understand how it feels because you had been living in a single parent home all through your teens. This is a quick way to set the foundation for a lasting relationship.

Develop a sense of curiosity when it comes to strangers. Emotionally intelligent folks are intrigued by strangers and always have an insatiable hunger to know more about them and understand their lives and views. They make an attempt to understand how the opinions and perspectives of these people are different from theirs. You know what to do next time you're on the train or at the airport. Immerse yourself in a different culture by traveling to various destinations whenever you can. It broadens your understanding of people and cultures. Sometimes, the only way to have an open mind is to go to a different destination and establish connections with locals.

## Day 17: Spend Time Away from the Social Media

Though this is the age of the social media, try and balance your online time and connections with offline relationships too. It is important to maintain face to face relationships with people since it paves the way for developing better social skills. Don't go messaging people. Instead, meet them over dinner or drinks and have a real, face to face conversation. Emotional intelligence goes beyond social media confines and needs real-world connections. Our ability to identify, process, and manage emotions is impeded by instant messaging and social media. Emoticons don't build emotional intelligence. It expands when we actually get out there and interact with people face to face. Staying in the constricted space of social media doesn't allow you to experience real emotions that can increase your emotional perception and intelligence.

## Day 18: Avoid Complaining

Complaining is a huge sign of low emotional intelligence. It happens when a person believes he is victimized and that the situation is beyond his or her control. They will pass on the blame to the next person or situation before thinking it through.

Emotionally intelligent people think in a constructive manner to resolve the issue rather than blaming someone else or complaining. They operate from a mindset that seeks to resolve the problem rather than working from the perspective of just making complaints.

Complaining is a huge sign that people believe they are mere victims of a situation and that the solution is beyond their reach. We consider ourselves victims of other people or circumstances and therefore are unable to find solutions to pressing issues. We believe that the solutions to the circumstances enveloping us are beyond our realm of control. An emotionally intelligent person seldom believes himself or herself to be a victim. They rarely feel that problem resolution is beyond their control. In place of blaming something or someone, they approach the matter in a more constructive manner and look for a solution quietly. Emotionally intelligent folks will peacefully contemplate an issue and look for a resolution through reflection and consideration of all possibilities in lieu of the current circumstances. There is a sense of maturity in their thinking and manner of approach.

The next time you are tempted to blame your alarm clock for waking up late and showing up late at work, resist the urge and focus on what you can do to wake up on time each morning. Can you cut down on post work partying? Can you watch less television and go to bed early instead? Can you set the alarm on two clocks, so you have a back-up if one conks out? There are many ways to resolve the issue if you get out of the victim zone and start looking for proactive solutions that are within your control.

Sonja Lyubomirsky's research has suggested that 50 percent of our happy state of mind is influenced by factors that are beyond control (genes, personality, temperament). The other 50 percent is influenced by a combination of multiple factors such as attitude (over which we have full control). Practice celebrating joy even in the most seemingly adverse situation.

## Day 19: Focus on How You Say it

What you say is important, but how you convey it is even more vital. There are multiple ways to say the same thing or handle a situation. Non-verbal communication can have a massive impact on how you are perceived by people.

Eye contact, voice, tone, expressions, and body language all contribute towards creating an impression about you among other people. It conveys to others how you are thinking and feeling emotionally. Think whether your body language and emotions complement each other. Are you able to articulate your emotions or feelings without offending the other person?

Keep in mind that few things destroy an individual's morale quicker than an overly critical person. Think of different ways to say something without affecting the other person negatively. I always recommend learning something about the other person or understanding them before attempting to communicate with them. For instance, if someone is particularly sensitive, they may not appreciate a direct, straightforward approach. You may have to get your point across in a more diplomatic and tactful manner.

Similarly, straightforward folks may not appreciate you beating around the bush. You may also have to employ a more frank and forthright approach. Thus, knowing an individual's personality will help you communicate with him or her in a more effective manner.

How you say it makes all the difference while communicating, especially on slightly tricky topics. For example, let's take a scenario where you think an employee is not suitable for a specific department and has consistently underperformed there despite receiving the best training, development, and mentoring.

As a manager, it is your responsibility to inform him that he or she is going to be shifted to another department. Now you are placed with the conundrum of telling them the truth without affecting his or her morale. What approach would you take as an emotionally intelligent person to accomplish the same?

Instead of telling the person that he or she isn't good in 'XYZ' department and that he or she is being shifted to another department, you can focus on the positive of the situation and change the angle or approach to give it a more positive twist. You can say something like, "We think you have the ideal skills for (new department) and that your skills or qualities will be utilized to the fullest there." You are still telling the employee that he or she will be transferred to another department, but you are putting across your point in a manner that doesn't offend them or lower their morale. You are simply telling him or her that their skills aren't being utilized to the fullest in the current department instead of telling him or her that their skills are not good enough for the current department. The words, body language, and approach make all the difference.

Also, active listening is a huge component of emotional intelligence, especially during conflicts. Often, while arguing with people, we have our responses ready even before the other person finishes speaking.

During heated discussions, arguments, and conflicts, we only listen to reply but not to understand the other person. How many times have you heard the other person out to truly understand them and not to prepare your response to what he or she is saying? Resist the urge to come across as too overpowering during a disagreement and try to understand where the other person is coming from. Deal with issues in a respective, productive, and assertive manner, without an element of defensiveness. When you actively and empathetically listen to the other person, you are also creating a space for your feelings and emotions to be heard. When you listen intently to the other person's views, you drain all the toxic energy from the situation and instead focus on arriving at a beneficial solution.

I always recommend practicing your non-verbal skills at home to make yourself even more clear and transparent in social situations. Start at your home because it is a space that doesn't make you feel overwhelmed, unlike an alien setting. Make a video of yourself interacting with a friend or relative.

Watch it so you can know what areas you can improve in when it comes to non-verbal signals. Another super way is to practice before a mirror. Pretend that you are interacting with a person and watch yourself in the mirror. Enlist the help of trusted folks when it comes to gaining valuable feedback. They can offer helpful insights about your voice, posture, expressions, and more. You'll be in a more private, low-stress setting, which reduces your shyness and preps your confidence for more important interactions. It's actually enjoyable to try out multiple gestures, expressions, signs, and postures.

When you can read non-verbal signals passed by others, you can quickly spot the disagreement in their feelings or emotions and words. Even a subtle mismatch in verbal and non-verbal signals will help you understand the other person's feelings and behavior.

Notice how sometimes you pick up some clue and call it a "hunch" that something isn't right about what the person is saying. What we like to call or think of as a gut feeling, or hunch, is actually a subconscious notice of the mismatch between the person's body language and words. The person didn't intend to communicate it, but we tuned in to their body language and "listened" to it.

## Day 20: Practice Assertiveness and Expressing Challenging Emotions

An essential part of being who you really are is asserting or being able to speak frankly and openly about things that truly matter to you or are important in your life. Practice taking a clear position on where you stand when it comes to vital emotional issues. Draw clear lines about what is acceptable and not acceptable in relationships.

Setting boundaries in relationships is also a huge component of emotional intelligence. It isn't restricted to being empathetic and being nice to others. Emotional intelligence is also about being fair to yourself.

Set clear boundaries so others can know more about your position which leads to lesser misunderstandings in relationships. This can include anything from disagreeing with someone about establishing priorities, to saying no, to protecting yourself from physical harm or mental duress.

Use the "I feel...when you" technique to assert yourself in tricky situations. For instance, "I strongly feel that I deserve a promotion from the organization based on my performance and contribution."

Similarly, when you are not comfortable doing something for someone over your own priorities you can assert yourself saying something like, "I don't feel comfortable that you expect me to do everything for you over my tasks and priorities." When you feel disappointed that someone doesn't follow through or listen to your instructions, you can articulate it with something like, "I feel really upset or disappointed that you didn't update me about the project despite being instructed to do so."

The trick is to say how you feel when something happens. Refrain from beginning your sentence with "you." It makes you sound accusatory and judgment. The moment the other person hears "you," he or she will subconsciously slip into a defensive position. You are quickly allowing the listener to assume a defensive position, followed by a bunch of excuses. If you want people to listen to you, talk about how you feel when they do something.

## Day 21: Reduce Stress and Practice Staying More Lighthearted

Stress rears its ugly head in all ways of life and completely consumes us following a range of negative emotions. From relationship breakdowns to being laid off from work, there are plenty of emotions that can overwhelm us. When you are stressed, it is challenging to behave reasonably. It will be tough to be emotionally intelligent when you are under tremendous stress.

Find what your stress triggers are and make a list of everything you can do to relieve yourself of that stress. What is it that helps decrease your stress? A long lonesome walk in the midst of nature? Listening to soothing music? Talking to a trusted friend? Having lunch at your favorite café?

Enlist the help of a professional therapist if it feels too overpowering to handle it by yourself. A psychologist, counselor, or therapist can help you cope with the stress in an effective and professional manner, while also helping you raise your emotional quotient. It is easier to establish rewarding interpersonal relationships with people when you are not under stress.

I personally love to combat stress by maintaining a lighthearted atmosphere at work, home, and other social scenarios. It is simpler to appreciate the joy and beauty of life when you take on a more humorous or lighthearted approach. It makes others around you feel less stressed too. Optimism and positivity not just lead to better emotional health (for yourself and others) but also more opportunities. (Who doesn't like being around a positive and optimistic person?) People are naturally drawn to optimistic, lighthearted, and positive people. Negativity, on the other hand, builds defenses. People with high emotional quotient use lots of fun, jokes, and humor to make the atmosphere for others (and themselves) safe, joyful, and happy. Laughter is indeed the best medicine to get through challenging times in our life.

# CONCLUSION

Thank you for getting a copy of *Emotional Intelligence: A 21- Day Step by Step Guide to Mastering Social Skills – Improve Your Relationships, and Boost Your EQ*

I sincerely hope you enjoyed reading it and were able to learn minute aspects related to emotional and social intelligence from it. I also hope it offered you plenty of practical ideas, helpful tips, and quick pieces of wisdom for increasing your emotional quotient and enjoying more fulfilling relationships.

The best part about emotional quotient is, unlike intelligence quotient, it can be improved through regular practice and implementation. Improving your emotional intelligence is a continuously evolving process that will keep getting better with time.

The next step is to go out there and use all the tried and tested strategies in the book. You certainly won't transform into an emotionally intelligent overnight. However, if you apply the techniques mentioned in the book in your daily life consistently and gradually, you are likely to see results!

You may slowly change from an emotionally challenged individual who struggles with emotions and social relationships into an emotionally evolved and socially adept person, who will enjoy more gratifying interpersonal relationships.

Finally, if you found this book useful in any way, a review on Amazon is always appreciated!

# COGNITIVE BEHAVIORAL THERAPY

*30 Highly Effective Tips and Tricks for Rewiring Your Brain and Overcoming Anxiety, Depression & Phobias*

# INTRODUCTION

Congratulations on getting a copy of *Cognitive Behavioral Therapy: 30 Highly Effective Tips and Tricks for Rewiring Your Brain and Overcoming Anxiety, Depression & Phobias*. Cognitive Behavioral Therapy can be an extremely effective means of dealing with a wide variety of mental health issues, primarily in the areas of anxiety, depression, and fear associated with phobias. What's more, there are plenty of exercises that you can practice yourself, so that you have a heads up when you start a more formalized therapy program.

Working through your personal issues without a guide isn't always a straightforward process, however, which is why the following chapters will discuss everything you need to know in order to get started on the right foot and ensure that your time spent with CBT is as effective as possible. First you will learn all about the principals at play in CBT, what to expect from the process, and how to tell if it is right for you. Next, you will learn about a variety of basic CBT exercises that will prime you for the more complex parts of the process and ensure you get off to the best start possible.

You will then learn about the various types of exposure therapy and the types of issues it is best suited to solve. From there, you will learn all about the many ways you can successfully deal with cognitive dissonance and persistent negative thoughts. Finally, you will learn about specific CBT techniques related to conquering anxiety, anger, or less harmful bad habits that are, nevertheless, extremely annoying.

There are plenty of books on this subject on the market; thanks again for choosing this one! Every effort was made to ensure it is full of as much useful information as possible. Please enjoy!

# CHAPTER 1

# ALL ABOUT CBT

Originally developed as a means of helping those who are dealing with depression, Cognitive Behavioral Therapy, or CBT, is a type of psychotherapy that has proved extremely successful, so much so, that its usage has been expanded to treat additional mental health issues including many types of anxiety disorders and the fear associated with extreme phobias. Essentially, the goal of CBT is to help patients control their personal issues by first changing the thoughts that cause the issues in the first place.

CBT utilizes aspects of behavior therapy as well as cognitive therapy and posits the idea that not all behaviors can be controlled with conscious thought alone. As such, there are many different types of behaviors that are built layer upon layer over time through a mix of long-term conditioning as well as internal and external stimuli. This means that CBT differs from many types of therapy in that it doesn't worry about the hidden meanings behind the things you do and the thoughts you think; instead, it focuses on doing what needs to be done to get the results you are looking for. As such, it tends to be the most effective for those who come to it with a specific problem they are looking to solve rather than a general desire for therapy.

This, in turn, will make it easier for the CBT-trained therapist you choose to figure out the best course of action for you moving forward. Issues including depression are considered to be a mixture of harmful stimuli and an equally harmful fear avoidance response. Issues that CBT is known to positively affect include psychotic disorders, dependence, nervous tics, addiction, eating disorders, personality disorders, anxiety disorders and mood swings. While CBT isn't for everyone, it is known to present a marked improvement over some other forms of therapy including psychodynamic options. Really, when it comes down to it, whatever works best for you is the best type of therapy. Ask a mental health care professional if CBT might be right for you.

A significant part of CBT has to do with the spotting and analyzing of what are known as cognitive distortions. First popularized by a pair of scientists named Kanfer and Saslow, the idea of cognitive distortions is now used by both therapists and computer programs as a means of shining a light on the many common, yet thoroughly inaccurate beliefs that people—and machines—are prone to make on a regular basis. This includes things like jumping to negative conclusions, minimizing the impact of positives, putting too much emphasis on the negatives, and applying results from isolated incidents to a wide variety of scenarios.

Many of these distortions are based on over-generalizations of one type or another, often associated with some time of discriminatory thought or false belief. CBT is especially useful in allowing those who follow through with treatments to become more aware and mindful of the limits their distortions place on them in an effort to minimize the effects of the same. Every person's psyche is going to be made up of a mixture of learned behaviors, if-then statements, and assumed emotions, not to mention the coping skills that were learned to force everything else to work together as best as possible. When you factor in the fact that any one of these could be warped in such a way that it has lead to a negative adaptation, it becomes easier to understand the work CBT has cut out for it. Ideally, however, it will take these distortions and replace them with positive alternatives instead.

## CBT History

Some exercises used in CBT have been in semi-regular use for thousands of years, such as the first recorded use among the Stoic philosophers in ancient Greece. They understood that logic was extremely useful when it came to determining which beliefs are true and which are false, and that understanding the difference was crucial to living an efficient and happy life. This idea is still one that drives modern CBT practitioners when they seek out issues that present themselves as negative thoughts and actions.

*Cognitive therapy and behavioral therapy:* Modern CBT can trace its roots back to behavioral therapy, which gained popularity in the 1920s thanks to the famous Pavlov's dogs experiment. This led to the idea that automatic behaviors can be trained based on external stimuli and was adapted for therapy by 1924 when a scientist named Mary Cover Jones started using it to help children deal with particularly robust fears. Behavioral therapy continued to gain acceptance throughout the 30s and 40s, and by the 1950s, it was one of the main types of therapies used to help individuals with these types of issues.

Meanwhile, in the early 1960s, a therapist by the name of Aaron T. Beck was working with associative therapy when he had a breakthrough about the nature of thought. Specifically, he realized that all thoughts are not formed unconsciously, which gives some the power to generate real, emotional responses as a result. This led to the creation of cognitive therapy in an effort to learn more about automatic thoughts.

*Coming together:* While behavioral therapy is great for numerous specific neurotic disorders, it isn't especially helpful in allowing patients to deal with their depression successfully. As such, by the 1960s, it had begun to be used less frequently, even as cognitive therapy really began to gain popularity. However, both types of therapy were already focusing on similar behavioral aspects to their treatment programs and also tended to focus more exclusively on what was going on in the present rather than other popular forms of therapy. Eventually, tests were conducted to see just where the differences between the two started and stopped, and after that, a mixture of the two slowly became the norm. However, the two were inexorably linked when two therapists, Dr. Clark and Dr. Barlow, used a combination approach to develop an extremely successful treatment for panic disorders.

## CBT assessment

The goal of CBT has never been to catalog every single issue that a particular patient is dealing with in an effort to determine what type of officially sanctioned mental health issue they are dealing with. Rather, it is much more interested in looking at the bigger picture in order to determine the true root of the problem. The goal then can either be to reevaluate how you deal with certain situations and then respond to negative thinking, or possibly change the way you naturally view different types of situations overall in hopes of mitigating trigger behaviors or negative habits.

The average cognitive behavioral assessment is made up of five different steps.

- Picking out primary behaviors
- Analyzing said behaviors
- Looking more closely at negative behaviors in an effort to determine their overall intensity, how long they last, and how frequently they occur.
- Decide on the best way to correct said behaviors
- Decide how effective the treatment is likely to be.

## Stages of CBT

*Therapeutic alliance:* The therapists who work patients through a round of CBT treatment don't work with clients so much as they form what are known as therapeutic alliances with them. As such, instead of listening to their client's problems and making a diagnosis, the CBT therapist works with the patient to come up with solutions that make sense to both parties to deal with the problems that are presented as a normal part of the therapy. This isn't going to happen immediately, however; the first thing that is going to happen is a session where patient and therapist get to know one another in an effort to determine if they are likely to work well together.

During initial sessions, the therapist will also assess the patient's mental and physical states in order to more quickly get to the root of the current problems. The goal for the end of the first session should be for both parties to determine if they can create a positive working relationship to effectively deal with the issues in question. This alliance is a crucial part of a successful CBT experience which means that the patient needs to take a serious look at how they feel about the therapist to ensure that they are comfortable opening up to them as this is the only way that true change can occur.

If you are starting a CBT therapy session and do not feel comfortable with the therapist that you have chosen, it is important to break off the new relationship and find someone that you do feel comfortable with. CBT is all about building positive habits to replace the negative and stifling ones, and this can't be done if you can't think of you and your therapist being on the same team. If something about the situation seems as though it is not working out, don't be afraid to go back to the drawing board and try something else instead; the therapist may even be able to give you alternative suggestions.

*Control your thought process:* After you have successfully formed a therapeutic alliance with a therapist you are comfortable with and have determined which problems you are going to be focusing on, you will start working on numerous different ways to control your own thought processes. In order to do so, you will need to understand what causes you to think the way you do. As such, the early sessions you attend will likely include some delving into your past to determine how, if at all, it actually relates to the problems you are currently experiencing.

Individual thoughts and patterns that were created as a way of coping with things that you had to deal with in the past are known as schemas, and getting rid of the negative ones that are preventing you from reaching your full potential is crucial in maximizing your long-term success. Part of this process will involve coming to terms with your preconceptions, which means analyzing how you think about certain things and exploring the reasons why this might be the case. During this stage, it is also normal for the patient to receive homework in the form of different exercises that you need to practice in order to start reliably changing negative thoughts and actions. While this portion of the treatment officially has no set length of time, an entire CBT treatment program rarely takes more than sixteen weeks to complete.

*Practice:* Once you have a better understanding of the way that you think, you and your therapist will then begin looking more closely at the way your thoughts and actions interact with one another in order to create the types of patterns that promote positive, rather than negative, behavior. Practice is the name of the game during this stage, as only practicing them on a regular basis will aid you in replacing your negative habits with positive alternatives. You and your therapist will also discuss new exercises during this stage, exercises specifically designed to replace negative patterns with improved versions. The end goal for this stage is for you finally gain control over your actions.

*Final stage:* You will be ready to enter the final stage of CBT when you feel confident that you can successfully manage your personal issues without your therapist's help. This doesn't mean that you will want to stop your treatment, however; instead, it will mean taking on the responsibility of managing your exercises on your own and keeping yourself inline when it comes to keeping up with the structure you will have recently grown accustomed to. Unlike many other types of therapy, it is entirely possible to learn to practice CBT by yourself as long as you take the required steps to get to the point where you can monitor your progress on your own.

CBT can be successfully administered in a wide variety of ways, starting with setting healthy goals, refining existing coping strategies or creating new ones, finding effective relaxation techniques, or practicing self-instruction. It can also be used in group settings just as effectively as it can be used in one-on-one scenarios. It can also be either presented directly, provided for a specific length of time, or only used briefly to help deal with a single issue. In fact, once you get to know some of the more common CBT techniques you will learn that many other self-help books are really just practicing some version of CBT. Therapists who tend to focus on this type of therapy often also expose their clients to positive stimuli as a way of creating new patterns; alternately, they may place the focus more on considering how to change the current thought process.

## Common treatment

CBT is frequently used in situations where adults are aware of problems in their lives and have run out of more traditional alternatives. In scenarios like this, it has been known to successfully treat depression, anxiety, psychosis, phobias and schizophrenia. It is also effective at treating certain types of spinal cord injuries, fibromyalgia, and even lower back pain. Currently, it is also one of the most commonly used treatments for schizophrenia as well. In those who are under the age of 18, CBT is known to be an effective means of treatment for suicidal thoughts, compulsive disorders, body dysmorphia, stress disorders, and repetitive disorders. Currently, there are also ongoing studies looking into its efficacy when it comes to treating attention deficit hyperactivity disorder in people of all ages.

*Anxiety:* A common CBT treatment for anxiety is what is known as in vivo exposure. This type of treatment puts the patient directly into confrontation with whatever it is that causes their anxiety, whether it be a fear of being around other people or a fear of heights. The idea here is that by exposing a person to the things that cause them anxiety in the first place, it will help their minds to overwrite the maladaptive coping techniques they have been using up to this point, in real-time as they will need to come up with a new way to handle what is going on right here, right now. This process is often broken down into two parts. The first part, extinction, takes place when the old thought patterns starts to be held in less regard by the mind as it has proven to be less than useful. Next, the process of habituation begins, and a new, move effective, alternative will take its place.

*Psychosis, mood disorders, and schizophrenia:* The theory of cognitive depression posits that people tend to become depressed when a majority of their thought processes take on a negative bias. In individuals who are prone to depression, negative schemas start to develop early in life and are then reinforced on a regular basis.

This, in turn, leads negative biases to form based on existing negative biases that then ultimately tint the other person's entire worldview. Other common biases in those with depression include magnification, minimalization, abstraction, over-generalization, and random inference. Each of these biases can make it easier for those who are depressed to make personal inferences about themselves and the world around them that are based almost entirely on these negative, and self-perpetuating schemas.

When it comes to dealing with psychoses, CBT can be especially effective when it is paired with medication because it can be easily adapted based on the issues that each person is dealing with. It has proven especially helpful when it comes to both minimizing the chance of a relapse and also managing any relapses that do occur as effectively as possible. CBT exercises can prove to be especially effective when it comes to helping those laboring under them to question their delusions or hallucinations and help them test reality to successfully ground themselves in an undeniably true time and place. It is so effective that it is recommended by the American Psychiatric Association for these types of situations.

## Deciding if CBT is right for you

While each of the exercises discussed in the following chapters are going to be more effective for treating some issues than others, this doesn't necessarily mean you are going to find something to deal with your specifics issues here. In order to determine if CBT is a good fit for you, there are some questions you can ask yourself:

- Do you prefer focusing on your current problems as opposed to those from the past?

- Do you believe that talking about your current troubles is more useful than discussing childhood experiences?

- Do you consider yourself to be primarily focused on achieving your goals in as short of a period as possible?

- Do you prefer therapy sessions where the therapist is active instead of just a passive recipient?

- Do you prefer structured therapy sessions over those that are open ended?

- Do you feel willing to put in effort on your own to support your therapy?

If you answered yes to a majority of these questions, then CBT is likely going to be effective when it comes to helping you reach your goals. While the exercises discussed in the following chapters can certainly help you deal with your issues, it is recommended that you only attempt them by yourself after you have successfully completed a guided CBT session. While there are some exercises you will be able to successfully complete by yourself, you will find that you are far more successful with the help of a professional as opposed to going it alone. Additionally, if you are dealing with any issues that may be life-threatening, it is recommended that you seek professional help as soon as possible to ensure you don't become a danger to yourself and others.

## Getting the most out of CBT

If you like the idea of CBT and plan on trying it out for yourself, there are plenty of things you can do in order to ensure that you get started on the right foot. Preparing properly will not only help make the undertaking easier to manage, it will also make CBT more effective from start to finish as well.

*Know what you are in for:* While there are some things you won't be able to learn about your future CBT therapist until you are in the room with them, there is still plenty of research you can do early on in order to ensure they are at least going to be a relatively reasonable fit. This means you are going to want to seek out online reviews of the practitioner and also consider the types of cases that the therapist seems to take on most frequently. If you are looking for a couple's therapist, for example, a therapist who seems to work primarily with children is most likely not going to be the best choice. When in doubt, ask around; you will be surprised just how many of your friends and coworkers are seeking some type of treatment.

*Prepare for change:* Depending on the issues that you are dealing with, you and change might not get along terribly well right now. This is going to need to change, however, and the change will be unavoidable. CBT is about little more than change of one type or another, and you can rest assured that you will be pulled completely from your comfort zone before things are said and done. This is why you are going to need to make a promise to yourself that once you start your CBT sessions you will commit to them until they are finished. This is the only way you are going to see any effect from the process, as it requires you to commit to the process for a long enough period that new habits replace the old, negative, ones.

A big part of this means that if you find that CBT is not working for you right out of the gate, the best thing to do is going to be to try and approach it with a different attitude before abandoning it completely. If you have been tentatively open to CBT so far, for example, then you might find better success if you fully commit to the process for the remainder of your time in the program. In fact, studies show that simply making a commitment to the change that comes along with CBT at the start can make the entire process more than 30 percent more likely to prove effective in the long-term.

This is not, of course, to say that you should remain in CBT therapy forever; after all if you can't commit to the creation of new, positive habits, there isn't much that can be done for you. What's more, setting a firm end date at the start of your CBT sessions can actually make it easier to make difficult changes that you may otherwise find yourself putting off forever. It is important to consider the context that surrounds your plan for change before determining the timetable that might be reasonable to plan for your success.

*Be realistic:* While CBT can be extremely effective when it comes to improving specific aspects of your life, this can only be done if you take a hard look at your life and are realistic about the problems you are currently facing. This is not the time to sugarcoat things; look at your life with a critical eye, and determine just what it is you are up against. While this process will likely be difficult, it is the only way you can ever truly expect to see real improvement.

# CHAPTER 2

# BASIC CBT TOOLBOX

While there are different types of CBT exercises to deal with different issues, there are always going to be some core exercises that everyone is going to end up doing, regardless of what problems they are trying to correct. Not only will mastering these exercises help you to start to see the error of your negative patterns, they will make the exercises in the subsequent chapters both easier to undertake and likely more effective as well.

## Tip #1: Journaling

Even before you have gone ahead and found a CBT therapist, if you are planning on starting sometime soon, then you can go ahead and start keeping track of the experiences you have throughout the day as well as how you responded to them. You are going to want to use the ABCD model for describing your experiences.

First, you will list the activating event, including an explanation of the situation, with all personal bias removed; this should just state the facts. You will also want to make note of the first thing that crossed your mind when the event occurred, as this is likely an automatic thought, which means knowing it could be useful later. From there, you will want to write down any beliefs that came into play as well, starting with the type of negative thoughts you experienced. If possible, you are also going to want to write down the source of the belief as well.

From there, you should write down the relevant consequences that occurred from the way you handled the incident, both short and long-term. Finally, if possible, you are going to want to dispute your negative thoughts and replace them with alternatives that you could have used instead. It is important to get into the habit of writing in your journal at the end of every single day as almost every exercise described in the following chapters can benefit from having a more complete idea of what the relationship between various actions, events, and emotions might be.

When dealing with CBT, it is impossible to have too much information about what is going on in your daily life, and the more events you write down each day, the better. While initially you may have a difficult time remembering the finer details of the things that happen to you throughout the day, it is important to keep up the practice regardless. Over time, you will find that you are more easily able to remember these types of details, but until then, you may want to take notes after a noteworthy experience occurs just to be sure you get everything right.

*Tip #2: Mindfulness Meditation*

Mindfulness meditation is a useful tool for those practicing CBT as it can help you learn to acknowledge your thoughts without interacting with them directly. Mindfulness meditation is also useful; once you get the hang of it, it can be used practically at any time regardless of whatever else you are doing. Initially, however, you are going to want to block out 10 or 15 minutes where you can practice finding the proper mindset.

To start, all you need to do is sit in a comfortable position, though not so comfortable that you may be tempted to fall asleep. Next, breathe in deeply and slowly. As you do so, take the time to really listen to all the things your senses are telling you. Feel your lungs expand as they take in the air, and consider the way it feels flowing into your body. Is it hot? Cold? Does it taste like anything? Your body constantly provides you with far more information than you give it credit for; taking the time to listen to it fully will help you to get closer to existing in the moment—the true goal of mindfulness meditation.

Once you have reached a relaxed state, to remove the excess thoughts that are likely running through your head, you need to picture them as a stream of bubbles rushing by in front of your eyes. Simply take a step back and let the thoughts flow past you without interacting with them. If one of them catches your attention and draws you into more complex thought, simply disengage, and let it go. Don't focus on the fact that you were thinking about it because that will just draw you out of the moment; simply remain in that state for as long as possible. Eventually, this will help with the negative thoughts you experience in the real world as well.

In fact, with enough time and practice, you will likely find that you are able to maintain a mild meditative state even when you are otherwise focused on the world around you. This is known as a state of mindfulness, and it should be the end goal of everyone who is new to the meditative practice. Being mindful means always being connected to a calming and soothing mental state as well as one that is full of joy and peace, which benefits not just yourself but everyone around you.

Research shows that practicing mindfulness regularly can improve brain health as well as function, and starting young will ensure your brain retains more volume as you age. Those who regularly practice mindfulness will also find they have a thicker hippocampus and as a result have an easier time learning and retaining more information. They will also notice that the part of the amygdala which controls fear, anxiety, and stress is less active. With all of these physical changes to the brain, is it any wonder that those who practice mindfulness report a general increase in well-being and mood?

Beyond the physical changes, regularly practicing mindfulness has been shown to decrease instances of participants' minds getting stuck in negative thought patterns while at the same time increasing focus. This should not come as a surprise given the fact that a recent Johns Hopkins study found that regularly practicing mindfulness meditation is equally effective at treating depression, ADD, and anxiety. It also improves verbal reasoning skills as shown in a study, which found that GRE students who practiced mindfulness performed up to 16 points better than their peers.

## Tip #3: Affirmations

Repetition is also a useful way to bypass many of the negative filters that may have built up in your mind over time. Repetition will allow you to slowly change those filters without having to butt heads with them directly. An affirmation is simply a positive sentence written down multiple times throughout the day. A mantra serves the same purpose, but it is simply repeated in your mind instead. Both are great ways to clear the background noise of negative thoughts that may fill your head throughout the day and help you focus on the positive goals you are currently working on. Over time, these can actually create new neural pathways in your mind that are free of the negative thoughts that plagued your previous way of thinking. This is especially true of mantras, as with practice, you will find that your chosen mantra can essentially always be playing in the background of your mind, influencing your thoughts and actions at every turn.

Popular options include:

- Today, you are perfect.
- Forward progress! Just keep moving!
- You are the sky.
- I am attracting all the love I dream of and deserve.

- Follow my path to happiness.
- I am strong. I am beautiful. I am enough.
- I am grateful for my life so far and for what is to come.
- I am fulfilled.
- Less is more.

## Tip #4; Situation Exposure Hierarchies

This exercise involves putting all of the things that you find yourself avoiding because of your current issues on a list, and then rating each on a scale from 0 to 10 in terms of how much trouble the list item causes you. For example, someone with severe social anxiety might place asking someone out on a date at the top of his list with a rating of 10, but asking for someone to hold the elevator might be at the bottom of the list with a rating of 2.

It is important to be thorough when you make your list so that you don't have any serious jumps between numbers. The end goal of this exercise is to slowly work your way from the bottom of the list to the top so that each new activity slowly adds to your overall level of discomfort. The idea is that by the time you have mastered the activity, you will have become used to that level of your specific stressor, so you can more easily move on to the next one. As such, it is important to not get ahead of yourself and try and bite off more than you can chew at once. A slow and steady buildup is going to be far more effective than a dramatic spike all at once.

## Tip #5: Behavioral Activation

The theory of behavioral activation states that negative life events over a prolonged period of time can lead to scenarios where individuals do not experience enough positive reinforcement for a prolonged period of time. This, in turn, can lead to additional unhealthy behaviors such as social withdrawal, unhealthy drug use, or erratic sleeping patterns. These patterns might provide some amount of temporary relief but are ultimately just generating a greater number of negative outcomes.

When utilizing behavioral activation, you will want to find something you know you are good at and a way to demonstrate your skill on a regular basis. The positive reinforcement that you receive will then, slowly but surely, transfer over into other aspects of your life as well. This, in turn, will make it easier to replace your avoidance behaviors with something more productive and rewarding.

## Tip #6: Improved Breathing

While it might seem surprising, your breathing habits could have a lot to do with several different anxiety and phobia-based issues. The way that you breathe is going to directly impact the way your body functions, and taking in either to little or too much can quickly exacerbate other physical symptoms you may experience as a result of whatever the triggering event might be.

In order to help ensure this is not the case as much as possible, when you find yourself starting to breathe erratically, notice what is taking place and counter your natural inclinations by breathing in slowly for four seconds. From there, you will want to hold your breath for seven seconds and then exhale for eight seconds. Repeating this process for around five minutes should be enough to ensure your breathing remains natural.

# CHAPTER 3

# EXPOSURE THERAPY

Exposure therapy is a type of CBT that is often used to deal with issues relating to the responses generated by either fear or anxiety-inducing incidents. While in guided therapy, you will likely be exposed to a variation of whatever it is that makes you afraid or anxious until the negative response has been lessened to the point it no longer presents a problem. There are also several types of exercises you can work through on your own.

*Tip #7: Interoceptive Exposure*

This type of exposure therapy is particularly effective for those who are dealing with fear or anxiety related to feeling specific bodily sensations. Avoiding these sensations then leads to biased behaviors based on biased beliefs, which then lead to avoidance behaviors. As such, exposure to these types of bodily sensations, known as interoceptive exposure can be an important part of treatment, especially when it comes to panic disorders.

To practice dealing with the issues that particular sensations call forth, practice the following.

Breathing

- Rapidly breathe in and out, taking full breaths each time (1 minute)
- Hold your nose and breathe through a straw (2 minutes)
- Hold your breath (30 seconds)

Physical exercise

- Run in place (2 minutes)
- Walk up and down the stairs (2 minutes)
- Tense all the muscles in your body (1 minute)

Spinning or shaking

- Spin as fast as you can while sitting in an office chair (1 minute)
- Spin while standing as fast as you can (1 minute)
- Shake your head back and forth before looking straight ahead (30 seconds)
- Put your head between your legs and then stand up quickly (1 minute)
- Lie down for a minute and then stand up quickly (1 minute)

Unreality

- Stare at yourself in a mirror (2 minutes)
- Stare at a blank wall (2 minutes)
- Stare at a florescent light and then read something (1 minute)

*Tip #8: Exposure and Response Prevention*

Learning to gradually face your fears is one of the most effective ways to break out of numerous different negative thought cycles. Exposure and response prevention works by exposing yourself to whatever it is that triggers your negative responses in controlled conditions. It is also important to make a point of avoiding existing, unhelpful coping strategies that may have been developed over the years.

In order to get started, the first thing that you are going to need to do is to learn more about your fears, specifically the triggers that bring on any negative habits associated with your negative thought patterns. To do so, you should keep track of your triggers for a full week. If you experience a large number of triggers, you may find it helpful to limit yourself to just three triggers per day. You will also want to label how intense the response to the negative thought pattern was on a scale of 1 to 10. Finally, you want to make a point of writing down any strategies that you used to deal with your issues, regardless if they are positive or negative.

The next step is going to be to create a situational exposure hierarchy as discussed in the previous chapter so that you can prepare to start dealing with them one by one. If you have several issues that might benefit from this type of exposure therapy, then you should make a separate list for each issue you plan on dealing with.

With this done, you will then be ready to slowly but surely face your issues by moving up the list of things that trigger undesired responses while strengthening your willpower by not giving into the response you typically associate with the trigger. When moving through this exercise, it is extremely important to take things slow and only move onto the next thing once you have thoroughly conquered the previous trigger. Skipping ahead won't help you deal with your issues more quickly; it will cause you to bite off more than you can chew, possibly pushing your recovery back in the process.

While moving through the things on your list, it is important to keep track of your improvements in a journal, so you can look back and see how far you've come. This is especially useful if you have several different lists ready and waiting, as it will give you the confidence to push forward with the forthcoming lists more quickly since you will have proof of how successful the process can be.

Finally, when it comes to actually confronting your fears, it is important to ensure that you aren't engaging in subtle avoidance techniques while you are confronting your issues as this won't do you any good in the long run. If the first thing on your list is still too much for you to handle face to face, then you will need to go back to the drawing board and come up with a less intense first step.

*Tip #9: Imagery Based Exposure*

Depending on the issues that you are working through, you may find that exposing yourself to images related to the things that activate your triggers may be enough to help you to move in the right direction. This is especially helpful if your issues are related to settings or scenarios that are not easily accessible. When you have the pictures associated with your issue, you will then want to remember instances related to the pictures when you experienced triggers. The more vivid the memory, the better.

Really focusing on these memories and bringing yourself back to them as fully as possible is crucial to the success of this exercise. When you start, try and recall as much sensory information about the moment as possible. Don't just remember the moment; place yourself there, remember how the space looked, smelled, felt, and then place yourself in the moment and let yourself experience the emotion again as fully as if it was fresh.

Once you have worked yourself up to the emotional peak, you will then want to pause and consider the emotions you felt and the thoughts that caused them before reflecting on the behaviors they generated as a result. Then, you will just need to follow the chain of events to their conclusion and decide if what took place was helped or hindered by your response. With practice, you will be able to realize when similar events are unfolding around you, in real time, and respond to them in a more positive way as a result.

*Tip #10: Nightmare Exposure and Rescripting*

This type of exposure is designed to help you to face your nightmares, thereby removing the power that they hold over you. Nightmare exposure naturally works in tandem with a secondary technique called rescripting. Rescripting is typically used as a means to help deal with particularly stressful memories by changing how you perceive them. It can be extremely useful, regardless if the memory that is being rescripted is something that happened in real life or if it is only something that occurs in nightmares.

Rescripting is also known to be beneficial when it comes to dealing with more everyday negative experiences that lead to sadness or frustration. Studies show that this technique can significantly reduce the frequency of related nightmares if it is used properly and on a strict schedule until results are achieved.

In order to start using this technique, the next time you have the nightmare that is causing you issues, don't try and pretend like it didn't happen when you wake up the next morning. Rather, challenge it and confront what it might mean. Consider the following aspects of your dream:

What was the worst part of your dream? While this might be a difficult thing to confront directly, the only way you can ever expect to change your dreams is if you understand them. Even if you have been dealing with the same dream for years, you will be surprised how writing it down will help shape it and make all of the details stand out in your mind. Once you have fully described the details of your nightmare, the next step is applying the same descriptive methods to any real-life experiences that may be influencing your dream. Don't be stingy with the details here; the more possibilities you can come up with, the better.

Next, you are going to want to compare the two, taking special notes of their differences. When you are in a dream, there are often inconsistencies in the plot or the world that will give them away, but only if you are alert enough to look for them. Not only will looking at the differences between dreams and reality make it easier for you to disregard the issues that your dreams bring up, it will make it easier for you to notice them in your dreams and wake yourself up as a result.

Once you have a list of negative events that you experience in your nightmare, you should consider the feelings and experiences that you have during the nightmare. Try and make a list that is as complete as possible. With your list completed, go through each, one by one, and come up with a positive experience that you would prefer to have in its place. These alternative experiences should be as detailed as possible, including sensory data and descriptive imagery.

While writing all of these things down won't clear up the problem all by itself, it is a start. From then on, after you wake up from the dream, go through your list, and, over time, you should see the specifics of your nightmare changing.

# CHAPTER 4

# DEALING WITH COGNITIVE DISSONANCE

As discussed in Chapter 1, everyone experiences some level of cognitive dissonance from time to time. If you feel as though your thoughts are drifting further and further from the way the world really works, however, one or more of the following exercises may be useful.

## Tip #11: Notice Cognitive Distortions

If you ever hope to improve upon your cognitive dissonance, the first thing you are going to need to do is be aware of the most commonly experienced cognitive distortions. If you see yourself reflected in the following examples, don't worry; they are extremely common, and there is nothing stopping you from changing anything you don't like.

- All or nothing thinking occurs when you are unable to see the shades of gray regarding yourself. As such, if you don't succeed completely, you feel as though you failed.

- Overgeneralization occurs when you let a single negative experience color the way you expect every similar experience to play out.

- Mental filtering is the name given to the habit of finding a specific negative detail in whatever you are doing at the moment and allowing it to color your judgement of everything else that is going on, sort of like the way a drop of food coloring can color an entire cup of water.

- Discounting the positive occurs when an event has both positive and negative consequences, but the fact that there are negatives at all prevents you from seeing the positives.

- Jumping to conclusions is an easy mistake to make. This doesn't mean it is harmless, however, as assuming the worst without reason can make it difficult to make any positive changes at all.

- Fortune-telling occurs when you have feelings that tell you an experience is going to turn out badly, and you believe them despite the fact that they don't include any evidence.

- Magnification or minimization occurs when you take a minor part of an incident and blow it out of proportion, or take a good thing that occurred and treat it as though it doesn't matter.

These are only some of the most common cognitive distortions, and writing down your activities on a daily basis in a journal, as discussed in chapter 2, can make it easier for you to discover the ones that you are dealing with on a regular basis.

*Tip #12: Track Thought Accuracy*

Once you have a list of a week's worth of cognitive distortions you have experienced and the triggers associated with them, the next step is going to be testing each of the distortions you experienced to ensure they are removed from reality. For example, if you find yourself spending an excessive amount of time worrying about problems because you believe that it will help you find a solution, then once you realize this is something you do, you can put the theory to the test.

For the next week, all you need to do is track the number of times you spent worrying about future problems, and then see how many of those actually lead to positive solutions. If it is more than half, then great; you were wrong, and this thought wasn't actually a distortion. If your problem turns out to be real, however, then you can move on and take steps to correct it.

## Tip #13: Behaviorally Testing your Thought

Depending on the cognitive distortion you are dealing with, you may be able to prove or disprove it by taking matters into your own hands. For example, if you feel as though not taking breaks during the day helps you to be more productive, then you could spend a week working as normal, and then rating your performance at the end of the day on a scale of 1 to 10. You would then want to take a week to factor in breaks in your schedule and then compare the two at the end of the second week to see which is more effective. If your cognitive distortion isn't bordering on a full-on delusion, then being directly faced with the inaccuracy of it should be a good way to promote positive change.

## Tip #14: Evidence For or Against your Thought

If the cognitive distortions you are experiencing can't be easily put to the test in the real world, then you can put it on trial in your mind instead. In this exercise, you will serve as the prosecution, the defense, and the judge in hopes of getting to the truth of the matter. When you are serving to support both sides of the argument, you are going to want to look at things from a purely factual angle, leaving emotions out of the equation entirely. You will then want to come up with the most rational argument as to why the cognitive distortion is both true and absolutely incorrect. Finally, you should compare the two arguments and determine which is the more rational. Ninety-nine times out of one hundred, you will find that the more measured response is going to be the right one and the cognitive distortion only served to further exacerbate the situation.

With this done, it is important to act upon the information that you have gained, especially if you have determined that the cognitive distortion is invalid. Going through the process of determining the accuracy of a cognitive distortion is meaningless if you don't follow through on what you have learned. The change doesn't need to be immediate; after all, some distortions will likely have been with you for a very long time. However, as long as you acknowledge what you have learned and remain open to new experiences moving forward, you will find that your old cognitive distortions can give way to a new way of seeing the world.

*Tip #15: Break Common Patterns*

Finally, knowing what you now know, the only thing left to do is to break out of the patterns that have formed around the cognitive distortions you are trying to break free from. This is going to be much easier said than done, however, especially if the habits are extremely deeply ingrained. As such, you may want to start by changing small aspects of the negative habits before working up to a full-blown change. This will give your ingrained neural pathways some time to expand before jumping to something entirely new and different.

Remember, it takes about 30 days to build a new habit from scratch, which means that once you have reached the point where you are ready to give the old habit the boot for good, you should be ready to immediately start something new to take its place. Having a new habit to replace the old one with directly will give your mind something new to latch onto, giving it a place to put its focus while you focus on the more serious task of kicking the old habit to the curb. Keep in mind that forming a new habit is a chance to improve some aspect of your everyday life. Choose wisely and keep it up once you start. While the going may be tough in the interim, in just one month you will be settled into your new routine, and it will have all been worth it.

# CHAPTER 5

# DEALING WITH PERSISTENT NEGATIVE THOUGHTS

Regardless of the issues that you are dealing with, having to force yourself to keep it up despite ongoing and extremely persistent negative thoughts can make an otherwise inoffensive therapy session and subsequent related exercises seem almost impossible to work through. Overcoming negative thoughts can often be extremely difficult, simply because you are using your mind to change something that your mind is doing, but the following exercises should serve to make the whole process more manageable.

*Tip #16: Anchors*

The anchor model can be used to replace any negative belief with a more positive alternative instead. To understand the basics, picture a hot air balloon being held down by an anchor at each corner. The balloon can be thought of as the negative thought that is holding you back, and the anchors are the social consensus, emotion, logic, and evidence that are holding it in place. In order to release the balloon once and for all, you must replace the offending belief once and for all as well.

To get started, the first thing you will need to do is find the offending thought; this is as easy as running through the thoughts that are always with you and stopping when you get to one that hurts when you think about it. For example, if you are an artist, then a common pervasive negative thought is that you don't have what it takes to be successful at your craft. With the thought identified, the next thing you should do is determine what anchors are currently keeping it in place. To do so, consider the following:

- What events or evidence anchor the thought?
- What emotions are tied directly to the thought?
- Who are the people around you that reinforce the thought?
- What logic is locking in the thought?

Once you have tracked down all the specific facets of the thought in question, the next step is choosing a new belief to replace the old one. For the best results, you aren't going to want to pick something that is the opposite of the previous thought, as this is something that your mind might reject outright. For example, if you are feeling depressed because you believe you will never achieve your dream, changing your thought directly to "I'm going to achieve my dreams" is too big of a shift. Instead, something along the lines of "If I continue to work hard and persevere, I will reach my dreams" is both motivating and not so much of a major shift the mind will reject outright.

## Tip #17: Avoid Negative Thinking Traps

One of the hardest parts of removing negative thoughts from your mind is the fact that the more you try and remove them, the more you think about them, and the more entrenched they become. Many people think of negative thoughts sort of like unwanted hairs that can simply be plucked out of the system and discarded at will. Unfortunately, the truth of the matter is that when you actively pursue negative thoughts with this goal in mind, all you are really doing is giving them the full benefit of your focus, making it easy for them to take control of your perception and distort it as needed to justify their existence.

To understand why this occurs, it can be helpful to think of a negative thought as you would a coiled spring. The more the spring is compressed, the more energy it is going to displace and the more resistance it is going to place against the downward force against it. Likewise, when you make the mistake of trying to suppress a negative thought in this way, all that occurs is that an even greater counter force is generated as a result. Thus, the more you try and not think about it, the more prevalent it becomes.

Instead, a better choice is going to be confronting the negative thought head on and determining whether or not it has any legitimacy behind it. By confronting the thought head on, you take away its power and can finally see it in an accurate light. With this done, you can then either disregard it completely as it isn't worth thinking about, or come up with a more effective solution than simply worrying about it all the time.

*Tip #18: Practice Acceptance*

For this exercise, rather than trying to get rid of your negative thoughts, you are going to accept them as a part of you and respond accordingly. For starters, it is important to understand that your mind is generating these thoughts outside of your control and without your consent. While at this point you can't always control what thoughts you want to have, just realizing this fact is a step in the right direction.

For now, it is enough for you to take a stance as an observer; simply being aware of all of your thoughts is a big step forward. At this time, you don't need to react to your thoughts or pass judgement on them; simply use the techniques you learned from mindfulness meditation in chapter one to separate yourself from then as much as possible. This goes for negative thoughts as well; let them enter your mind and then leave again on their own accord. Do not resist them.

You may find it useful to think of each thought as an arrow; once the arrow is released, it accelerates until it reaches a maximum speed before then losing momentum moving forward. When it comes to negative thoughts, not resisting them will let them continue to fly until they have burned themselves out, while holding onto them, even to resist, will only cause their power to grow.

*Tip #19: Change your Belief System*

Another key step to banishing negative thoughts is to get at the source and remove negative thoughts that you have identified from your belief system. Specifically, this means divorcing your negative thoughts from your personal version of yourself by understanding that they don't reflect reality and are simply a product of an untrained mind. To start changing these thoughts, you need to express them in such a way that they are separate from yourself.

For example, if you are feeling anxious, you would verbalize this fact by saying, "I am having thoughts that I am anxious; this is just my mind telling me to feel this way and is not an accurate reflection of the current situation." You could then list all the reasons that come to mind as to why you do not currently need to feel anxious. By making the effort to complete this mental shift, you are distancing yourself from the negative thoughts, which then shifts them from automatic thoughts to active thoughts, thoughts you can more easily do something about.

Once they are in the realm of active thoughts, you can then use what are known as rational coping statements to plan how you are going to deal with these thoughts and feelings when they arise. For example:

"I am having the thought that I should skip working on my business goals. My mind is telling me I need to postpone making phone calls to potential customers because I usually get a lot of rejections, and that's a painful thing for me to go through. But if I am honest with myself, I know that if I don't make these phone calls and let these thoughts control my decisions, then I have zero chances for making new contacts to help my business grow. I know that reaching enthusiastic customers is not an easy thing to do, but when I do, I feel very proud of myself, and it makes calling them all worth the effort. I realize I have an option in making these phone calls, and if I look honestly at my schedule, I know I can find 20 – 30 minutes a day to make these phone calls."

## Tip #20: Writing and Destroying

If you find that your negative thoughts are typically linked to strong emotions, then you may find success, and catharsis, by getting them out in writing. For this exercise, you should get out a pen and some paper and physically write down everything that is bothering you. Be as verbose and specific as possible; try and get all of the emotion related to a specific thought out in one go; leaving anything inside will allow the thought to build up to the previous levels once more.

Then, once you have gotten out everything that you care to, you can then destroy the paper in any way you deem appropriate. If you aren't a writer, any type of physical representation of your negative emotions will do. This exercise is about getting the negative emotions and their related thoughts out of your mind and into the physical world where they can be dealt with more easily. Destroying the representation of the feelings shows your commitment to moving on and living your best life.

# CHAPTER 6

# CBT TECHNIQUES FOR DEALING WITH ANXIETY

Strong emotions arise before thoughts that are related to them are fully formed, not afterwards, as it likely appears when you look back on a particularly emotional incident. As such, you will often find that it is easier—and more effective—to change how you feel about a situation than what you think about a situation. As such, if you want to use CBT to help your anxiety, then the following exercises are a great way to work on calming your feelings directly.

*Tip #21: Focus on How your Feelings Change*

When working with CBT, it can be easy to get so focused on the way your feelings are currently aligned that it can be easy to forget that feelings are fluid, which means they are always going to be open to change, even after you have already put in the effort to work on them for another specific reason. Likewise, just because you spend a month or more working on your feelings of anxiety, doesn't mean that you aren't still going to get a little anxious every now and again. Rather, it is important to take the new anxiety in stride and see how severe it ends up being before you get too stressed out about it, possibly causing yourself far more mental strife than you would have had you just taken the small amount of anxiety in stride in the first place.

You may also find it helpful to verbally acknowledge how you are feeling in the moment and how you expect those feelings to change once the anxiety has passed. For example, you might say, "Currently I feeling a little anxious, which is natural given the situation. When the feeling passes, I anticipate feeling clear headed and calm once more."

Additionally, you may find it helpful to keep a close eye out for the first signs that the feeling is passing and the anticipated change is about to begin. Not only will focusing on the anxiety being over actually make the end come on sooner, it will also stop you from reacting poorly to the anxiety in the moment. Feelings always shift, and keeping this fact in mind may be enough to push things in the right direction.

## Tip #22: Act Normally

While generalized anxiety disorder is considered a mental illness, anxiety itself is a useful survival tool when doled out in moderation. It is only when things get out of hand that it goes from being helpful to harmful, sort of like an over-eager guard dog. The truth of the matter is that your anxiety response only kicks in because your body is responding to the current situation as if there was a threat. Regardless of whether or not the threat is real, a perceived threat is enough to set off the response.

As such, one way to train your anxiety to be selective effectively is to give it the type of feedback it understands so that it knows it is not currently needed. Anxiety takes its cues from what you do along with a basic type of emotional pattern matching, which means that if you act as though everything is currently normal, then the anxiety will back off and calm down. As such, you are going to want to do things such as maintain an open body posture, breathe regularly, salivate, smile, and maintain a calm and measured tone of voice.

If you can successfully adopt just one of these behaviors when you are feeling stressed, then you can successfully alter your feedback enough that your fear response, directly from the sympathetic nervous system, receives a message that says everything is fine. In fact, one of the most common ways of mitigating an oncoming feeling of anxiety is to chew gum. If you don't have any gum handy, simply miming the act of doing so is going to be enough to make you salivate, convincing your body that nothing interesting is going on.

The reason that this is so effective is that you would never have the luxury of eating a delicious meal during times of serious crisis, which makes your body naturally assume that nothing that is taking place is a legitimate threat. This, in turn, changes the feedback loop the body was expecting and causes the anxiety to retreat back into the background. Just knowing that you have this quick trick in your back pocket can give you a boost of confidence that takes you past the point where your anxiety would trigger in the first place.

Remember, anxiety functions based on the expectation of something catastrophic happening in the near future. All you need to do is prove that this is not the case, and you will be fine.

*Tip #23: Discover Underlying Assumptions*

As a general rule, if you feel anxious about a specific situation, then this is because you are afraid of some potential consequence that may come about as a result of whatever it is that is taking place. However, if you trace those fears back to their roots, you will often find that they aren't nearly as bad as you may have assumed they would be when they were just a nebulous feeling of anxiety.

For example, if you are anxious about attending a party, then looking inside to determine the consequence that you are afraid of might reveal an internalized fear of meeting new people. Tracing that fear back, you might discover that it is based around the consequence of other people not liking you, which you are determined to avoid due to issues in your past.

However, if you trace the consequence of people not liking you, then you may find that it makes you upset because it reinforces existing feelings regarding your general likeability. Once you get to the ultimate consequence that is causing you anxiety, you can look at the problem critically and determine what you can do to get to solve the issue that you are avoiding. In this instance, reminding yourself of people who do like you is a valid way to avoid the issues you are afraid of.

This exercise is also especially effective for those who are dealing with relationship issues, as they can clearly describe all of the fears they have associated with the relationship falling apart. In the process, they will come to understand that things will continue as normal after the relationship falls apart and that they will be able to move on if the relationship is not intact.

*Tip #24: Progressive Muscle Relaxation*

Another useful technique in combating anxiety is known as progressive muscle relaxation. This exercise involves tensing and then relaxing parts of your body in order. The reason for this is because it is impossible for the body to be both tensed and relaxed at the same time. Thus, if you feel an anxiety attack coming on, a round of concentrated tense and release exercises can cut it off at the source. Progressive muscle relaxation exercises may be done routinely or before an anxiety provoking event. Progressive muscle relaxation techniques may also be used to help people who experiencing insomnia and have difficulty sleeping.

To get started, you will want to find a calm, quiet place that you can dedicate to the process for approximately 15 minutes. Start by taking five, slow, deep breaths to get yourself into the right mindset. Next, you are going to want to apply muscle tension to a specific part of your body. This step is going to be the same regardless of the muscle group you are currently focusing on. You are going to want to focus on the muscle group before taking another slow, deep breath and then squeezing the muscles as hard as you possibly can for approximately five seconds. The goal here is to feel the tension in your muscles as fully as possible, to the point that you feel a mild discomfort before you have finished.

Once you have finished tensing, the next thing you are going to want to do is to rapidly relax the muscles you were focusing on. After five seconds of tensing, you will want to let all of the tightness flow out of your muscles, exhaling as you do so. The goal here is to feel the muscles become limp and lose as the tension flows out of them. It is crucial that you deliberately focus on the difference between the two states; in fact, this is the most important part of the entire exercise. Remain in this state of relaxation for approximately 15 seconds before moving on to the next group of muscles.

# CHAPTER 7

# CBT TECHNIQUES FOR DEALING WITH ANGER

In response to being ignored, criticized or overwhelmed, it is natural to feel angry, annoyed or irritated. In fact, as long as it is expressed appropriately, anger can lead to constructive change and other healthy coping mechanisms. Unfortunately, when the anger is not expressed properly, such as when outbursts are frequent, long-lasting, or particularly intense, then outbursts can be quite harmful.

It is important to keep in mind that anger, in this instance, isn't limited to showy displays of shouting and yelling, and internalized anger is often just as bad as externalized anger—and is potentially more harmful to the person experiencing it as well. It can also lead to more serious results such a self-harm or damage to property. Some people can even become trapped in cycles where they become angry, then they feel guilty about it, then they get angry again when someone brings up the previous incident. It doesn't take a rocket scientist to understand that excessive and uncontrolled anger can easily cause problems in all facets of life. It can lead to strained relationships with coworkers, friends, and family and maybe even issues with the law.

There are many different reactions to anger—both immediate and delayed. As an example, many people are far more likely to go out of their way to avoid someone who is angry all of the time as opposed to someone with a cheerful disposition. What's more, those who are angry on a regular basis are more than twice as likely to suffer from chronic headaches, heart problems, stomach issues, and more. Even more consequences of untreated anger can occur in the long-term. Those who don't deal with their anger issues could find themselves prone to mood swings and withdrawing from social situations. They also typically develop problems related to anxiety, self-esteem, and erratic drug use. Untreated anger has also been linked to instances of increased cancer cell growth.

Luckily, CBT is an effective treatment for excessive anger, as it can help you to understand when you are deflecting anger from the true source of the problem onto those around you. Nevertheless, before you try the exercises outlined below, it is important to keep in mind that anger is a natural emotion, and there are times when being angry is a perfectly valid response. Learning to distinguish between these moments and periods where your anger is uncontrolled, exaggerated, or associated with otherwise dysfunctional behavior is crucial to improving all areas of life.

Additionally, you will need to remember that the behaviors that you exhibit are patterns just like any other, which means that they have been developed, reinforced, and repeated countless times throughout your lifetime. When you add to this the fact that anger is an automatic emotional response, it is important to factor in an appropriate amount of time before you see results.

Finally, when it comes to dealing with your anger issues while in guided CBT therapy, it is important to keep in mind that there are many different approaches to doing so. Some individuals may find success by exploring the experiences that cause them to become angry, while others might need to look at the issues that lead to anger as an automatic response in the first place. Regardless, the following techniques have proven to be helpful for many individuals dealing with a wide variety of anger related issues.

*Tip #25: Increased Personal Awareness*

Many people tend to lose focus when they become angry to the point where they don't have a clear sense of the boundaries of their anger. They don't understand where it is coming from or what exactly is taking place that makes them angry. Once again, a journal will help to ensure you are moving in the right direction—just make sure you are writing in it every day, or even multiple times per day if you find you have trouble recalling everything clearly at the end of the day.

When chronicling your angry episodes, it is important to ask yourself the following questions:

- When do I find myself getting the angriest?
- Where do I find myself getting angry most frequently?
- What situations am I in most often when I get angry?
- What events tend to trigger my anger?
- What sorts of memories tend to trigger my anger?
- Are there any images that seriously trigger my anger?
- How do you feel physically when you become angry?
- What is your emotional state like when you are angry?
- What thoughts frequently move through your mind when you are angry?
- How did you handle the situation that made you angry?
- Is the way you behaved during the most recent time you were angry par for the course?
- If so, why? If not, what made this time special or unique?
- What is the general response like when you get angry?

By answering these questions, you will become more aware of the results, reasons, and nature of your anger, which will go a long way towards allowing you to develop a more well-defined sense of self-worth, while also improving your self-control—two things that should go a long way towards improving your ability to handle anger in a healthy fashion.

When journaling, it is important to keep track of the times that you did not become angry, despite experiencing triggers, just as you did those times that you did become angry. While the two types of experiences are often going to be quite different, when you do see overlap, you will be able to analyze the two events side by side in order to determine what it is that allowed you to keep your cool in one situation while losing it in the other. While an increased awareness of the reasons behind your anger is useful, it is likely only the first step towards improving your anger once and for all.

*Tip #26: Anger Disruption*

Disruption and avoidance techniques work by removing yourself from the anger causing situation, either physically or mentally. While this might be as simple as getting up and leaving the room to prevent yourself from blowing up at the person you are speaking to, things won't always be this simple, or leaving the room might not be a realistic option for one reason or another. At the very least, you are going to want to give yourself time to think things through and delay the need for a response by asking the other party for time to think about whatever is causing the issue or to verify your information before continuing.

You may even decide that it would be wise to continue the conversation via another medium entirely such as email. Not only will this provide you with the time you need to cool down before explaining yourself, it will ensure that when you do, you have all your ducks in a row and will be able to elucidate on your points clearly and effectively. Regardless of the path you choose, giving yourself the time you need to calm down is crucial to shorting out the pattern of anger that you are falling into when you get into a yelling match with another person face to face. Taking some time and getting some space will make both of these far easier to avoid.

*Tip #27: Cognitive Shift*

When you get angry, it will often cause you to make already bad decisions that much worse simply by the way you view them in your mind. This, in turn, often leads to one or more types of negative, limiting thoughts that make it less likely that the angry person will be willing to come to any type of compromise. As such, the next time you are angry, try stopping for a moment and reframing the situation in a more moderate way. While this won't always lead to a tenable solution, simply considering it should be enough to cause your mind to stop being angry and start being productive.

If you can't get yourself out of that angry mindset, silly humor might be able to get you there. Silly humor isn't about laughing all your problems away; rather, it is a type of cognitive reframing technique that can help cut your anger off at the source. For example, if you find yourself getting angry during rush hour traffic, instead of referring to the other drivers by unflattering derogatory statements, find a silly image and refer to the other drivers by that description instead. If you can make yourself laugh every time you say it, you likely won't remain angry for long.

# CHAPTER 8

# CBT TECHNIQUES FOR BREAKING BAD HABITS

While CBT can be used effectively for a wide variety of serious mental health issues, that doesn't mean that it can't also be useful for those who aren't dealing with anything so serious but still have a few bad habits that they want to take care of once and for all. Habits are a core part of life, and it would be almost impossible to function without the hundreds of them that likely allow you to make it through the day without consciously thinking about every step in every task that you complete successfully. Everything from driving to work in the morning to making dinner in the evening is based on habits, and without them, our lives would fall into disarray.

However, if you have unpleasant or annoying habits, then CBT can be utilized to remove them, just as it would be with any more serious issue. And just like any more serious issue, the first step is going to be making a conscious effort to change, starting with becoming more aware of just where and when the habit is taking place. Only once you have discovered the patterns that are associated with the habit will you be able to actively work to alter it for the better.

*Tip #28: Develop a Stop Strategy*

Bad habits are simply patterns that your brain has developed over time. Once you have been studying the behavior for a prolonged period of time, you should have a better idea of what can trigger it. As such, when you find yourself about ready to interact with one of these triggers, add the new habit of saying stop before you do whatever it is that would have triggered your need to go through with your bad habit. If simply saying stop doesn't seem to be enough to get your mind to do what you want it to do, you may want to write STOP on a piece of paper with your signature and then take a picture of it with your smartphone so that you are sure to always have it on you.

If saying or seeing the word stop doesn't seem to be enough, perhaps you can enlist the aid of a friend who can step in and cut off the habit before it gets up and running. Anything that you can do in order to break your body of getting into the habit is to be encouraged. If you don't seem to be seeing any success at first, or if your habit actually seems to get worse, the most important thing you can do is to not give up. Instead, you should consider how long it took you to build the habit up to its current state and give the process a little extra time to start working.

When you are able to dissuade yourself from participating in the habit that you are trying to break, it is equally important to celebrate this fact. Rewarding yourself each time you are able to successfully avoid following through on your habit will not only give you the motivation you need to keep it up when the going gets tough, but it will actually make it more likely that you will be able to succeed again in the future. This is because rewarding yourself will be enough to make the memory stand out in your mind, which will, in turn, give you a new focal point outside of the traditional habitual activities that take place and lead to the same old responses to the same old stimuli.

*Tip #29: Try Alternatives*

Until you are completely free of the behavior in question, you may find it helpful to occupy yourself in such a way that you cannot follow through on the habit in question while you are doing it. This is why so many smokers either take up chewing gum or develop an oral fixation while they are trying to quit smoking cigarettes. It is important to do more than simply replace one habit with another, however, as even if the new habit is an improvement, there is no guarantee you won't revert back to the previous habit if you had to give up the new alternative.

Rather, once you have successfully switched to the new, less damaging habit, consider the feelings that it generates as a result. With any luck, the new habit will promote the same feelings as the old habit, allowing you to get to the root of your desire for the habit in the first place. Once you have done so, it will then become much easier to determine how to best go about fixing this issue in the first place.

Once again, it is important to work on being as consistent as possible when it comes to replacing one type of habit with another. If you are persistent in switching them out, then you may find that you have simply developed a new habit, without actually clearing out an old one. As such, it is important to only undertake this type of exercise if you have the time to closely monitor the habit at all times as this is the only way you will be able to weaken it successfully.

During this period, you may experience feelings of disappointment and stress as it feels like nothing is happening, but it is important to understand that this is natural. Do not let it keep you from continuing to strive for your goals. When you feel your resolve slipping, simply keep thinking of all the benefits that breaking the habit successfully will provide you with, and remember that changing your habits is a marathon, not a sprint; slow and steady wins the race. You may find that this is another instance where rewarding the times that you successfully alter your habits leads to additional success. Changing habits is hard work; don't be afraid to reward yourself as needed.

*Tip #30: Manage Lapses Effectively*

Habits have a tendency of reoccurring right up until the time that they are broken completely. Even then, if they aren't removed from your mind completely, they may re-emerge without warning; they are, after all, automatic. As such, it is important that you take your bad habits one at a time and focus on them until they are purged from your neural pathways. If a lapse does occur, it is important that you do your due diligence and determine why it occurred and figure out what you can do to ensure that it doesn't happen again. Remember, if you manage to successfully master a habit once, there is no reason you can put down the lapse as a simple slip and go about your business as normal.

When it comes to dealing with lapses of this sort, it is important to never use them as an excuse to fall back into bad behaviors, even for a short period of time. It won't take much to reactivate old neural pathways, and allowing them to regain their foothold will only make it more difficult to move forward successfully when you are finished indulging your moment of weakness. Starting down this path is a slippery slope to destroying all of your hard work.

# CONCLUSION

Thank you for making it through to the end of *Cognitive Behavioral Therapy: 30 Highly Effective Tips and Tricks for Rewiring Your Brain and Overcoming Anxiety, Depression & Phobias*. Let's hope it was informative and able to provide you with all of the tools you need to achieve your mental health goals. Just because you've finished this book doesn't mean there is nothing left to learn on the topic; expanding your horizons is the only way to find the mastery you seek.

CBT is a living, breathing specialty, which means that the longer it has been since the publication of this book, the more likely there are new alternative strategies on the market as well. Don't rest on your laurels; ensure you are dealing with your mental health issues as effectively as possible. Likewise, don't forget that practicing these techniques on your own is in no way a substitute for the wisdom and guidance a professional CBT therapist can bring to the process. Don't limit your success. Complete the process properly.

When it comes to using the CBT exercises discussed in the previous chapters successfully, the most important thing of all that you can remember is that practice makes perfect. Perhaps more so than any other type of therapy, CBT involves creating new habits and sticking with them in order to replace the negative, faulty, habits that caused you to seek out this type of therapy in the first place. As such, once you get started, you need to be ready to see things through to the very end. While you certainly have your work cut out for you, the results you seek are possible, and all you need to do is want them bad enough and not stop until you have achieved your goals.

Finally, if you found this book useful in any way, a review is always appreciated!

# MINDFULNESS

*How to Create Inner Peace, Happiness, and Declutter Your Mind*

# INTRODUCTION

Thank you for getting this book, *Mindfulness: How to Create Inner Peace, Happiness, and Declutter Your Mind*. Congratulations on taking the first step toward living a life of mindfulness.

Taking charge of your life, and making the decision to live the way you would like to, is a big deal. By choosing to live a life with more meaning, one that makes you better connected, you are off to a great start toward the mindfulness that you seek. The peace you will gain while learning to live a life of mindfulness is priceless. Well wishes to you on your journey.

There are plenty of books on this subject on the market, thanks again for choosing this one! Every effort was made to ensure it is full of as much useful information as possible, please enjoy!

The following chapters will discuss the idea of mindfulness, and things that you can work on to create inner peace, add happiness, and remove clutter from your mind in an effort to be more mindful in your everyday life. This book is a step-by-step guide to get you on the right track, and with a feeling of true inner peace. By using the advice and suggestions in each chapter, you will begin to notice a change in the way you see the world. The chapters in this book are organized in a manner that begins by bringing your attention inward, which is where this journey must start. In order to truly live a life of mindfulness, one must start within themselves. Once the inner self is more at peace, addressing the other aspects of becoming mindful will be much easier to accomplish. The chapters then work outward to address the world around you and discuss the approaches you can take to make your way through the world more mindfully.

While reading this book, it is important to keep an open mind, an open heart, and be honest with yourself. Mindfulness is a process, and this book will lead you through that process. The journey will be more fulfilling if you approach it with every intention of learning more about yourself, and the world around you. This book will help you to view your world through new eyes.

Before you begin this book, prepare by finding a calm, quiet place to read. Give yourself the time to read as much as you would like, and allow yourself to feel at ease as the pages turn. A suggestion would be to read one chapter at a time, taking notes if you feel it is helpful, and process the information from each chapter before moving on to the next. There are several activities throughout the book that suggests writing or recording things electronically. So, you may want to get a journal or your note taking method of choice.

The mindfulness you seek begins now.

# CHAPTER 1

# CREATING INNER PEACE

As was mentioned in the introduction, a journey toward mindfulness begins from within. Inner peace is a thing we hear about often, but may feel is outside of our reach. Many people talk about it, and seek it out, never knowing that the search itself may be the very thing that is keeping them from attaining it. Trying so hard to control the external world in an effort to gain inner peace seems to be a common method, yet it is counterproductive and only creates more turmoil. The first step to inner peace is letting go. There are several other elements to help one obtain peacefulness, but letting go is foremost. Creating inner peace is mostly an understanding between yourself and the world that you are who you are, and the world is not in control. Everything that occurs outside of you only interferes with your inner peace when you allow it to by reacting to it.

That's right; you control your inner peace with how you react to the things that happen in your life and in the world around you. In this very important chapter, we will address this, and work on the things you can do that will help you have a better grasp on inner peace.

Let's begin with old business. Although the focus in this is introspection, one cannot leave things unresolved from a time when inner peace was not a priority. Things from the past that may still be a source of turmoil for you must be put to rest. Having things unfinished will feel that way until you finish them. They will continue to interfere in your journey to mindfulness and need to be resolved.

Apologize to whomever you know you should. Make amends with whomever you can, even if it's only for the sake of your inner peace. Tie up the loose ends that you may have left at schools, old workplaces, old living situations, and any other relationship of any kind. Most importantly, forgive everyone. Once you have forgiven, you take away any power those issues have over you. It is empowering and freeing to let them know you have forgiven them, in any way you are able. It helps everyone involved, and you can mark that off your list forever. Resolve each of the open-ended contentions, and settle up all of your affairs. This will ease you into acceptance.

Letting things go will become easier the more you do it, and you have already practiced surrender and acceptance by resolving lingering matters. Now you can take it a step further by deciding to completely accept all things that you cannot change, and surrendering to what is. This does not mean to throw your hands up in the air and give up. There is a finesse required to keep from crossing the line between accepting and just checking out. Acknowledgement is the key to acceptance. You must first let yourself be aware of the things you cannot change in order to surrender and truly accept them. An example of this could be spilled milk. You can ignore it, and decide not to let it affect you, but it eventually will by becoming a rotten, stinky mess. When you notice the spilled milk, accept that it was spilled, and surrender to the fact that you must clean it up and move on; you eliminate spilled milk disrupting your peace and keep yourself from a more difficult and odious problem in the future.

This leads us to the next element of finding inner peace, and it's a biggie. Choose your own behavior, and take responsibility for your actions and reactions to the world. Decide who you want to be, and put forth an effort to maintain your inner peace in any possible situation. Other people, places, and events do not make you behave any particular way. You are not a puppet. You are in control and are ultimately responsible for how you express yourself. Decide to take full responsibility for your reactions to the world around you. It's important to trust yourself with the information given to you, solicited or not, and slow your reaction time so as to decide how you would like to react, or whether to react at all. Self-control is a very big part of choosing your own behavior, and practicing it will make it easier to give yourself the time to remember who you have chosen to be and make a choice in how you respond.

Of course, this does not mean you are a perfect stoic tower of tranquility at all times. Taking responsibility for your actions and reactions means that no matter what your response is, you claim your part in it. None of us is perfect, even people on the journey to mindfulness. When the outside world does its thing, we will sometimes receive that information, forget to take the time to remember for ourselves who we want to be in every situation, and human nature takes over to produce a reaction from us that we may not be proud of. That's ok. We must accept it, take responsibility for it, and address the feelings that may have gotten us to that place.

Addressing the feelings you have will lead you to become perceptive and aware of all feelings, yours as well as those of others. Figure out what pushes your buttons, and try to understand why those things are triggers for you. Hard to face, and otherwise uncomfortable feelings come with a message, and it is important to your inner peace that you acknowledge and attempt to understand them. A good way to do this is to metaphorically hold the emotion in your hands, and examine it. Ask yourself where this feeling might be coming from. Why do you think you are feeling this? Is there an underlying cause? Take note of whatever you discover, allow yourself to feel that feeling, accept it, and let it go.

Once you've learned to be more aware of feelings, you can work on honesty, with yourself and others. Telling the truth is a very important part of attaining inner peace for several reasons. For one, it keeps your mind free. There are no lies to remember as well as no guilt weighing you down. Another reason honesty is important is because if you aren't being truthful with yourself about things you need to let go, those things won't hold any meaning if you've sabotaged the process by altering what the real focus needs to be. Lastly, being truthful will assist in your journey to inner peace by allowing you to say what you really feel and think. It is very liberating to genuinely express yourself, and your world becomes a lot more simplified when you aren't constantly juggling how your feelings may affect others while attempting to anticipate their reaction to them. Learn ways to tell the truth while still being kind. Your integrity will take you much further than the instant gratification a lie provides.

Integrity will be a positive side effect of your inner peace, and knowing your higher self comes along with it. When you get to the emotions behind the reasons for your reactions to your external environment, it will ultimately bring you to ego, and lower consciousness. Just by recognizing this, you are living as your higher self. We all have ego, and we all have to work with it, but taking the time to examine ourselves and learn about the driving force behind how we interact with the world puts us on the path to inner peace. Distinguish between your true self versus the outward personality you share with the world. Most likely, the person you show to the world is a combination of ego, your surface level needs, and past experiences. Take the time to explore the person you really are, and begin to let your veritable self come forth. What are your values and ideals? What brings you joy? What are you passionate about? The answers to those questions are what define you; this is your authentic self.

The detachment from your false self and keeping your ego in check will go more smoothly if you begin to slow down. There is no place for overworking, winning, outdoing, or competing when mindfulness is the goal. Move more slowly, take the time needed to complete tasks, and make an effort to not feel rushed. Everything we do takes time, and giving yourself time to do things in a deliberate manner means that you are more peaceful while moving through your day. Give up the fight, and sit it out while you gain invaluable inner peace.

Slowing down may cause you to begin to notice small imbalances in your life that had previously been overlooked. It is important that you give these matters some focus, and address them as needed. They are your opportunities to practice what you have learned. When you sense a disharmony, acknowledge that you cannot change everything, examine the discord, separate yourself from it, and address it in a healthy way. You will become more sensitive to damaging influences, and get better at handling them with a sense of mindful tranquility.

When you make inner peace the priority, your focus becomes clear. Implementing the skills you now have can bring you to a place of inner peace more quickly and easily the more you make it commonplace. Your inner peace will become a predominant fixture in your everyday life once you decide for yourself that it is.

# CHAPTER 2

# CREATING HAPPINESS

In this chapter, we will discuss what it means to create our own happiness. If you feel as though creating happiness is a pipe dream, it's a good opportunity to use what you learned in chapter one. What made you feel as though you cannot create happiness? What past experiences brought you to the place where simply suggesting you can create happiness seems ridiculous? Examine those feelings, decide where they come from, acknowledge and address them, let them go, and take back control of your joy.

Maybe you feel as though you know what will make you happy, but think you can't attain it easily. It is common knowledge that most people think they know what will make them happy, and then once they've gotten it, they realize it was not the answer. This has happened since the dawn of time, and it all stems from the fact that happiness is not a goal to be met by an outside influence. Happiness comes from within. This is why one man can be happy with nothing, and another can be unhappy with everything. The man with nothing has found his happiness in a way that is not attached to accomplishments or things. He is truly happy in his heart, with or without the outside world. A happy soul has joy whether the list is marked off or not. They are not waiting for something to make them feel happiness, because it is with them at all times, in all situations.

You create your happiness when you let go of the things that keep you from it, and concentrate on the things that bring you to it. Decide that happiness is a part of the person that you are. Know that when something makes you unhappy that it will be short lived, and you will be able to bring yourself back to a feeling of happiness. Experiencing setbacks and hard times is a part of life, but self-directed positive action is the key to bringing things back to good. One thing you need in order to do this is a list of things that make you feel happy to revisit when needed. The list is an ever-evolving, very fluid register of both the simple and the complicated things that make your heart swell. This list is quite literally your happy place.

What has ever made you smile? What has made you cry with joy? What brings you laughter through tears? Get a pen and write them down, or put them in a note on your phone. Put them on an index card to keep with you, or place post-it notes all around your house as constant reminders. Your list can have people, places, things, memories, stories, instances, and smells, anything that has brought you happiness and still does. These are your building blocks. The things on your list are your comparables. These are your lighthouses in the night, and you will use them when you lose your way. The list of things that make you happy is also your constant reminder that you create the happiness in your life, just like you created that list. You decide, and every situation can be a happy one (eventually) if you just make it that way. You determine your destiny; you are the bearer of your happiness.

You create everything in your life. That's a hard pill to swallow, and some will argue the validity of that statement, but it's absolutely true. Everything you see before you now is of your will, and the outside influences are of little to no consequence. Your thoughts and feelings become your reality because they are the basis of everything. Just like your actions and reactions to things, your thoughts and feelings create the world around you. Your view of people and situations is under your control, and what you decide about everything makes it what it is to you, good or bad. We already discussed how your reaction to everything is your decision, and how you feel about it is, as well. Thoughts become things. Your feelings become your reality.

Start right now; take this very moment to feel happy that you are reading this book. Know that this moment is perfect, and you are exactly where you are meant to be. Close your eyes for a moment, and feel your heart beating, your lungs breathing. Now decide to feel happy about it. Feel happy that your heart beats, that your lungs breathe, that you can comprehend the words of this book. Recognize that these are actually great things in your life, and feel gratitude for them. Let the happiness flow through you. You may notice other happy thoughts pop up. Acknowledge them, and give them the time to flow through you, as well.

Congratulations, you just created your own happiness! All you have to do is take it a step further, then another, then another, until you have helped yourself to discover as many happy things as possible, and it has filled your life for most of the hours of most of the days. Happiness isn't something that happens to you, it is always something you create. It always has been. Everything on the list you made makes you happy because you decide that it does. If you handed your list to someone else, they might not find happiness in your pet fish, your favorite plaid socks, or the memory of ice cream with your grandpa. Those things hold the joy that you have decided for yourself.

Creating happiness is the same as creating anything else; you simply bring it into existence. The best way to put oneself in a place that creates happiness is to feel love. When we feel happy, what we are actually feeling is love, and that avenue can go both ways. Feeling love for something brings us happiness, and when we need to find happiness, we only need to feel love to get us there. If listening to your favorite music makes you happy, it's actually your love for the music that you are feeling. When spending time with loved ones brings you happiness, it's your love for them that is bringing about that feeling. Even something as simple as laughing at a joke is based on love, your love for that particular kind of humor. The key to creating happiness in your life is love. When you feel love (happiness), it grows, and when you genuinely give love (happiness), it comes back to you ten-fold. This is where all happiness and joy stems from, and this is how you create it. It takes some practice, but a good way to begin is to start small. When you find yourself feeling happiness, recognize that it is love, and really let yourself feel it. Notice the feelings you are experiencing, and embrace it. Feel grateful for that moment, and remember what it was that brought you to that feeling. Then when you have the need to bring happiness to yourself, you can revisit that moment and put your mind in that place, the place of love, where you feel happy. Just like that, you have created happiness in your life.

There are other, less abstract ways you can create your own happiness if you are really having a hard time getting started. These things can be used as a starting point if you are struggling to put yourself in a place of feeling or expressing love.

Remember to look at the list that you made of tried and true people, places, things, and situations that make you happy. Look at each one of the things listed, and one by one think about them intently. Feel the love that comes from them, feel the happiness in your heart. Know that how these things make you feel is your true state of being. You love all of these things, and they put you in a place to feel nothing but goodness and joy.

Stay away from negative people. People who complain and are otherwise overall negative people can keep you from creating your happiness because they most probably wallow in their problems and fail to focus on solutions. Misery loves company, and they need others to join their pity party so that they are not suffering alone. You may feel obligated to listen to the bellyachers because you don't want to be seen as heartless or rude, but there's a fine line between being a polite person, and getting immersed in someone's negative emotional state of mind. You can avoid getting sucked in by setting boundaries and distancing yourself. A great way to stop them in their tracks is to ask them how they plan to fix their problems and share any ideas you may have. The negative person will hopefully feel better, and you have now redirected the conversation to a place of productivity.

Make a list of your accomplishments, no matter how small you may think they are. Did you wake up this morning? That alone is an accomplishment. Being a human is hard work, and living through every day as a productive member of society takes a lot of effort. Once you've listed all of your basic accomplishments from square one, move on to other things you have worked to achieve. Have you graduated from anything? Have you won any awards or promotions? Have you created artwork, music, or crafts at one time or another? Do you have a family or any strong relationship you hold dear? All of these things are just a starting point. The possibilities for things you have accomplished are endless. Once you have a list, look at each item on it and remember how it felt when you succeeded at them. Feel the happiness that came from completing that task, and see if helps you to notice happiness in other parts of your life.

One good way to discover love and happiness in your life is to spend time with a friend or family member, for no reason other than to visit with them. Have fun; even maybe enjoy an activity together. Take work, and the need to accomplish something out of the equation. Maybe even just sit with them, and talk about anything and everything. Learn about their desires, what makes them happy, and feel genuine love for them. Feel happiness for them in their ongoing journey through life, and feel grateful that you have that person in yours. When you leave from your visit, reflect on the things that made it so great, and remember all the reasons why that person and the things you do with them make you happy. Pay attention to the emotions you feel when thinking about them, and take note of where they come from. Perhaps you can't pinpoint why this person makes you happy, and that's fine. Just remember that they do, and that's a great place to start.

Another thing you can do to create happiness is to volunteer. If you feel the need to accomplish a goal, this will feed it, without the ramifications of a selfish reward. When you volunteer your time and effort, the effects of your conscientiousness spread further than yourself, and are felt more strongly. Selflessly helping another person or animal will automatically put you in the place to feel love, and create happiness in your own life. You can volunteer at churches, soup kitchens, food pantries, nursing homes, schools, humane societies, and even children's homes. Searching the internet is a great place to start when looking to volunteer. While you are volunteering, feel love and happiness toward every person and animal you encounter. Take note and remember times when you feel particularly connected or an abundance of joy. Then, when you leave the place you decide to help at, take the time to reflect on your experience, and perhaps write down those instances. Examine those feelings, and extract the parts that translate to happiness for you.

Creating happiness will begin to come naturally to you when you express love freely and make happiness a way of everyday life. Happiness is not a goal you will reach by attaining other things and accomplishments. Happiness is love, and it grows where you plant it.

# CHAPTER 3

# DECLUTTERING ONE'S MIND

The world is a full and vibrant place overflowing with constant stimulation and chaos for our minds. There are lots of wonderful new things coming at us every day, new ideas, new ways of thinking, and new things to make us feel like maybe we aren't enough. There is also a great deal of noise, stress, worry, and responsibility that we face just to live day to day. Simply looking up a recipe on the internet becomes a circus, and we are inundated with advertisements, social media notifications, text messages, emails, and more thoughts than our brains can process; all of that just because we wanted to make some onion soup. It's easy to get jumbled, and side tracked in the world today, and it's very common to have a cluttered mind.

In a journey toward mindfulness, it is important to take stock and dump the clutter. Just like with the other chapters, it's time to take charge and decide that your mind is just that, yours; and you oversee the state of it. Feeling restless and unfocused are not conducive to mindfulness. We will learn how to take out the useless junk and make sense of most of what's left. This will help us to obtain the calm our mind so desperately needs.

The mind is a very complicated place, full of both useful and useless information marred with the scars of old hurts and past traumas, as well as the memories that make us who we are and what we know. There are countless levels of consciousness that are impossible to sort through. So, in order to remove the clutter, it's important to keep it simple and take a deep breath.

Breathing is actually a great place to begin. Intentional breathing is a well-known practice that helps one focus and clears their thoughts. Normally, we don't think about breathing, it just happens automatically. When breathing intentionally, the idea is to concentrate on the breaths, bringing your focus back to the core of your being, your life force, one of the most basic things your body does. Close your eyes, take a deep breath in through your nose, deep into your lungs. Fill your lungs, let your belly expand, and then exhale slowly out of your mouth, all the while concentrating on your breath. This exercise will center you.

You can declutter your mind by concentrating on simple actions. When you're doing anything, even the most mundane tasks of your day, be present. This helps to remove all of the other noise happening in your mind, and brings you to a place where there is only one thing going on. Look closely at the task at hand, and really notice every part of it. Direct all of your senses to what you are doing. When washing dishes, brushing your teeth, folding laundry (anything you usually zone out while doing) focus intently on your actions, and feel gratitude for the ability to do it. Look at your hands, say to yourself, "I am so fortunate to have these dishes and the food that I ate them on". It can even get as basic as being mindful of the hands you are fortunate to have in order to wash the dishes. Concentrating intently on simple actions will help you to successfully remove the clutter and only focus on what you have happening in that very moment. This is decluttering at its best.

Somewhere in the evolution of time, it became socially favorable to multitask. This has taken the mindfulness out of everything and attributed to the endless clutter in our heads. Multitasking and constantly thinking of what we need to do next is helpful at times, but it is important to not make it a habit. To live life in the future, and have your mind elsewhere will only make you miss the part you're living now. This is where most of the clutter comes from, to begin with. When I'm eating my dinner with a to-do list in my head along with the plan for the rest of the night weighing on my mind, and the stress of the electric bill and the leaky faucet tangling up with those thoughts, I give myself no room to be thankful for the food I'm so lucky to be eating. Being present in my current situation is where I find my mindfulness anyway. So it works two-fold to eliminate the clutter and keep me living in the now.

A way to get all the extra jumbled up clutter out is to write it down or keep track of it electronically. Life comes with a lot, and if you aren't putting most of it somewhere else to revisit at the appropriate time, you're constantly keeping a running list in your mind. It is much more conducive to conscious living to have a written list and schedule than to expect yourself to remember everything in an ongoing fashion. It's exhausting and creates tons of mind clutter to keep a running loop of reminders in your thoughts. Put them somewhere else, and decide on a time to address them. Set yourself free from all of the ongoing responsibilities of life being a part of every moment, and give them a moment of their own at a time when you can be fully aware and present. It will only make taking care of these things more successful because you can give them the attention they deserve. So write down your thoughts, lists, responsibilities, problems, and other life situations that need your acknowledgement; and when you do, mark your calendar for when you will address them. Just like that, you have eliminated the need to have many things cluttering your mind; as well as encouraged your inner peace.

You will realize very quickly that giving one thing attention at a time may mean that you need to eliminate some unimportant baggage that has been attributing to the clutter. It's time to identify the essential. Your essentials are what are secondary to everyday living. Obviously, brushing your teeth and eating, all basic living mind stuff that comes with being human goes without saying. What are the non-negotiable residents of your thoughts? If you were to dump the contents of your mind, what would be the first things you would grab back? The essential parts of your mind are what are most important for you to focus on. Make a short list of these things to feel confident that you are aware of them, and even when you declutter your mind, they will not get lost.

Now that you have identified the indispensable, what is not essential will begin to stand out. What things in your mind are not necessary or important to you? Better yet, what parts of your life are not good for you? What feelings, behaviors, or thoughts are just there for no reason other than you've grown accustomed to them being with you? Eliminate these things, and give your mind a lot of wiggle room. The emotional baggage that comes along with these useless matters is just extra space that can be opened up; and by now, I'm sure your decluttering is really beginning to be noticeable.

It is a great idea to become familiar with journaling if you haven't done so already. Keeping a journal is a way to make sense of all of the work you are doing toward living a mindful life. You have now written a couple of lists, done some elimination exercises, discovered new things about yourself and gotten rid of a lot of emotional baggage that goes along with the process. Addressing these things in depth may help you to explore areas that you aren't aware of, and assist you in discovering mind clutter you didn't even know was there. Writing in a journal about your pilgrimage to mindfulness may be something that can help you to process this large amount of feelings and information, and contribute to ultimately letting go of what no longer serves you.

A few other things you can do to help declutter your mind are to get plenty of quality sleep, participate in physical activity regularly, and cut down on screen time. Our televisions, phones, tablets, computers, and other electronic devices are constant streams of information inundating our minds. Take time every single day to turn off all electronic devices and unplug.

Spending time with nature will make you feel more in-touch. We are natural, organic creatures. We began our evolutionary cycle much more a part of nature, and being in it can bring us back to a place of calm. Take a walk outside, go to the park, or sit by a body of water. Listen to the wind blow, and feel it across your skin. Interact with the trees and watch the birds. Take your shoes off and place your feet in the grass or water. Remember that the earth is an unbelievably giant place, and we are just one small part of it. Lie down on the ground and look at the sky. Feel the enormity of the earth under you while you look at the giant sky that has no end. These things will help to eliminate the effects of unnatural light and being indoors, as well as eliminate clutter from your mind.

Declutter your surroundings. It is very important that wherever you spend your days is clean and free of chaos to create calm. You cannot sit in a room full of clutter and expect to rid your mind of clutter. Take a day to remove excess stuff from your living space, and organize things. Purge your surroundings of unwanted things, or items you no longer use. Donate them wherever you see fit and reap the rewards of a cleaner place, and the good feeling of giving your old stuff a new home.

You can also try to practice meditation, which is a proven method of clearing and centering. Meditation has been around since the dawn of time, and even if you feel intimidated by it, it's a great way to clear your mind of clutter. You can do it anywhere you can find a quiet space. If you need them, there are even guided meditations of all sorts on the internet to help you get started. There are meditations with music, sounds of nature, talking, relaxation techniques, even with bells and flutes. Anything you find calming has most probably been incorporated into a type of meditation. They call it "practicing" meditation because there is no such thing as doing it perfectly. Simply closing your eyes and concentrating on your breathing is a form of meditation, and you can do it as little as one minute to begin to reap the benefits.

CHAPTER 4

# BEING MORE AWARE

While reading the past three chapters you have been put in positions that force you to be aware. They have widened your eyes and awakened your consciousness. You may not have realized it, so let's think about what "being more aware" actually means.

For one to be aware indicates that they are in a conscious position of perception. They are processing the information being given to them through their five senses and acknowledging it. To be aware is to realize and recognize. If the goal is to be 'more' aware, then we work harder at it. Being more aware can happen immediately, and we already touched on it in previous chapters. When you decide to be present and live in the now, you are more aware.

It takes practice, and you can start small. In order to feel more physically aware, just feel your body, where you're sitting, where your feet are, notice where your hands are positioned. Now move further from yourself to your external surroundings. What do you see? Who is in the room with you? What lights are on? What sounds do you hear? You are becoming more aware, and can now look back to yourself and feel the difference in your consciousness. You are here, now, and can feel fully present and aware of yourself.

When it is taken further, increasing your awareness involves your beliefs and principals. Are you aware of your deal breakers? What are beliefs that you hold true, and can you define your moral compass? The answers to these questions are essential for being more aware because you must know yourself before you can know anyone else. Being more aware takes integrity and understanding so that your perception is not warped. Become aware of how your actions affect others, as well as yourself. Everything you do has a kick-back, and in a journey toward mindfulness, it is detrimental that you are aware of what it is. When you are conscious of the effects of your actions, you become more mindful of the things you are doing. Just the act of paying attention to the words that you use will bring you to being more aware. What you put out becomes a part of the world in one way or another, and being fully aware of what you are contributing to the world around you is a big step toward a more mindful life.

Being more aware takes an open mind and an open heart. There is an understanding that comes with awareness that is invaluable. The best way to become more aware is to look at every situation as if every other being you encounter is you. Not that they are just like you, that they actually are you. See things from their point of view, and try to understand what they may be aware of. Imagine if we are all connected, and each of us is a part of one big thing. We can call that thing the Universe. It is us, we are it. In order to be fully aware, we must acknowledge that we are all the same. So when we look at some other part of the universe, rather than it being separate from ourselves, we are aware of its place in the grand scheme of things, and that place is within us.

# CHAPTER 5

# ELIMINATING STRESS

I know, I know...easier said than done. But look how far you've already come in this process! You've already eliminated some stress, so we are simply taking it a step further.

When you decided on your essentials, you made a list of what was non-negotiable for you. That list contains the most important things in your life, your bottom line. You also made the conscious decision to let go of emotional baggage and mind clutter that no longer serves you. In doing that, you eliminated stress. We can now work on removing it from other areas.

Stress comes from mental and emotional strain caused by unfavorable or challenging circumstances. Sometimes a little stress can be good for us. It can push us to try harder or improve upon ourselves. When we are attempting to live a more mindful life, stress is not in the equation. Eliminating all the stress we can is detrimental to our health and well-being, and must be done in order to live mindfully. Now is the time to make yourself, and your stress level a priority in order to keep this journey less complicated. Nothing can be done thoroughly and efficiently under stress, and making others aware of your intentions is one way of bringing down your stress level.

Sometimes, your friends and family are a source of stress for you simply by being in your life, because their stress can become your own. You have to decide that you will not let their troubles become a source of agitation for you. It is possible to be comforting and understanding without taking on other people's problems. If you are eliminating stress, the first worries to go need to be those of others. You are not able to change their circumstances by feeling emotional strain. It has never worked, and it never will. So let the stress of others go. When you are approached with another person's stressful situation, take the time to acknowledge what they are sharing with you, and let them know that their feelings are important. If a way to eliminate their stress comes to mind, share it with them, if you like. Let them know that you hope the best for the matter, and treat them with kindness. If you find that their troubles come back to your thoughts, recognize that this is simply you feeling empathy, and let them know that they are on your mind. Maybe you can even ask how things are, and if they have resolved the matter. Keep yourself from actually feeling the stress, because it could possibly help them more in the long run, anyway. Your mind free from stress works more efficiently, and with all of the decluttering you have been doing, perhaps you will come up with a viable solution to their problem. Eliminating stress has a ripple effect, just like a lot of the other things you have learned thus far.

Now we are back to self. One of the most prevalent causes of stress in human beings is finances. Some would say money is the root of all evil. I say it is the bane of peace; but only if you allow it to be. Take most of the stress surrounding finances out of the equation by making everything you can automatic. We live in an amazingly effortless time where automated systems and paperless billing are commonplace. Wherever you are financially right now is what you are working with, so just make as many of these financial responsibilities as little a part of your everyday life as possible. Work with your financial institution and others to set up all that you can to be automatically deposited, paid, withdrawn, and recorded.

Designate one day a week to check into things to be sure they are in good working order, but don't keep this plan in your daily thoughts. Write the weekly financial check down on your schedule like you have learned, so that you truly remove this part of the stress of finances from your thoughts until it's time to address them. Getting your finances in order, and putting the responsibilities associated with them in a safe place to be revisited takes the thinking out of it for the most part, and gets rid of that portion of stress.

Another source of stress is the everyday, mundane tasks that do not deserve the amount of significance they get. Back to the idea of auto-pilot, what other routine things can be put in that mode? Ask yourself how you can eliminate stress for each part of your day simply by taking the guess work and over-thinking away. How does your day begin? What can you put on auto-pilot? Taking the stress out of your breakfast is as easy as planning the week ahead. This also helps your budget, and your waistline -both sources of stress. Win, win, win. Pick a day of the week to plan your meals and shop. You can even go so far as to prepare them. This provides the opportunity to start your morning with zero room for anxiety regarding your breakfast. You can do this for most of your meals, and eliminate all stress regarding your food, your shopping, even your diet. This is just one every day area that you have quickly eliminated all stress from. What other things can you plan ahead of time to keep your mind more stress-free?

When taking an assessment of your everyday life, you could discover that a portion of your stressful situations may have been coming from the cluttered mind you just worked so hard to declutter. So, some stress will fall away now having taken the time to eliminate the excess unwanted things you needed to. If you still find that you are stressed out on a daily basis, perhaps an overhaul of time management and scheduling skills are in order. Running late, for example, has a snowball effect, and can ruin your entire day. So can forgetting to get your oil changed, or missing an important appointment because you didn't write it down in your schedule. If these types of things are repeatedly putting you in a state of stress, take the time to work on your time management and begin to be better at writing down scheduled appointments. This may be a huge way for you to eliminate a lot of stress.

It is important to know that stress can come from all directions, and sometimes we cannot anticipate when it may become a part of our lives. We must learn to deal with it effectively, so as to keep it from disrupting our peace. If a stressful situation occurs, there are things one can do to change the stress into a different feeling that doesn't carry such detrimental effects. Evaluating the situation, stepping back and looking at the big picture, and remembering that this too shall pass is a perfect way to take back your power in any stressful situation. By helping yourself to realize the stressor is not bigger than you can handle, the stress fades away. It now has evolved into an addressable situation that you can separate yourself from and no longer feel a sense of urgency about. Decide to be cool as a cucumber, and even when your instinct to stress out takes over, you will remember to take control in order to eliminate the stress.

Perhaps you are feeling stress that is unavoidable due to your profession or extenuating circumstances, or maybe you feel stress that of which you cannot pinpoint the source. Yoga, the system of stretches and exercises intended to help one attaining physical and mental control along with a sense of well-being, is an outlet that can help to alleviate that stress until you can get a better handle on it. The philosophy of Yoga teaches the suppression of bodily activity as well as the mind and personal will. This is so that the inner self can realize its distinction from the physical form so as to gain mindfulness and awareness. Using stretches, controlled breathing, and relaxation, yoga can help lower blood pressure, improve circulatory function, and reduce stress.

## CHAPTER 6

# BEING IN THE PRESENT MOMENT

Although this seems like a no-brainer, it can really be a difficult concept to grasp. We touched on this when we discussed being more aware, and it is a significant part of being mindful. Being in the present moment is all about keeping yourself involved and in tune to what you are doing, and what is going on around you. If you are sitting around a campfire, watching the flames, listening to the story being told, looking at the people around you, the smiles on their faces, the stars in the sky, you are being in the moment. If you are looking at the flames and your mind begins to think of what time you want to pack up and head home in the morning because you have a deadline to meet on Monday, you are living in the future. Then again, if looking at the flames takes you back to camping with your parents when you were small, and this leads you to a drawn out episode of melancholy, you are living in the past. Some people do this sort of thing constantly, and it keeps them from being a part of their own lives. It is great to plan for the future and sometimes wonderful remember the past, but those moments should be short-lived and should be secondary when working toward mindfulness. Making the present moment in the forefront of your thoughts keeps you in a state of awareness that automatically leads to being mindful.

One state of mind that can prevent us from being in the present moment is feeling self-conscious. When other people's potential perception and judgment of us is forcing us to be fully aware of only ourselves, we fail to be in the present because we can't see past how we might look to others. We waste the moments of our lives that could be spent looking outward to see amazing things, looking inward with tainted glasses to beat ourselves up about not being good enough. Having confidence, or even lack of concern about what others might think, helps us to live in the current moment. Our looks, style, image, presence is no longer a worry, we can watch the show, and really pay attention.

Life unfolds in the present, and we can miss time as it goes unnoticed while we live in the past or the future. Some also tend to keep themselves from enjoying the current world by being jealous or envious. Comparison is the thief of joy, and when time is spent coveting another person's life, looks, or possessions, it is impossible to be in the present moment. Looking over the fence into someone else's yard puts you in a state of another reality. You aren't able to see what's going on in your world at the moment when you're busy wishing your grass was as green as theirs. Look at your grass, be thankful you have grass and notice that at least you can see all of the grass and other beauty surrounding you. If jealousy is something you find yourself feeling often, the best way to eliminate it is to remember that whomever you are jealous of is only on a pedestal because you put them there. Decide to stop giving them your attention, and make the only person you compete with yourself. Improve upon yourself, and jealousy fades away. Reading this book is a great place to start, so give yourself a pat on the back.

Our thoughts can control us if we allow them to. Having power over your thoughts is a great way to keep yourself in the present moment. Allow your thoughts to flow through your mind, and just be. Simply sit and listen to the nothingness, allowing yourself to be the most basic of human beings. Know that it is enough to breathe, and sit in the world. You can best be in the present moment when it is just you, and the moment. Stop doing, comparing, planning, regretting, etc. Step out of that ongoing wave of thoughts, and just rest in the stillness. Open up to the present moment, and intentionally focus on what is happening right now. Go back to focusing on breathing, and take in your surroundings. Consider going to a quiet place to connect to the present if you need to. Stop thinking about it, loosen up your mind, and just be. The present moment is all you have right now. Live in it. Soak it in. You'll never be in this same moment again.

# CHAPTER 7

# BENEFITS OF MINDFULNESS

When we make the decision to be mindful, we begin to do things with peace and love and create a reality based on the present. We are only truly living our lives when we are aware and perceiving the current moment. Our lives are intended to be used to the fullest; we are here to experience every emotion, feeling, and way of being. Deciding to be mindful is the first step; we must then decide it for ourselves every minute of every day, over and over again. Being mindful is a way of life with endless benefits.

What we think becomes our life. Living in the past gets us nowhere, and worrying about the future, or giving it too much importance, robs us of the present. If we are constantly thinking of what is going to happen next, we live in a state of uneasiness and aren't able to enjoy what we are doing. Likewise, living a life regretting the past, or feeling melancholy for times gone by, makes us unable to appreciate the present and move forward. As we have already discussed, our thoughts and feelings become our reality and being mindful keeps us in a place of giving and receiving all that is good.

The benefits of mindfulness are more than just peace of mind and a better way of life. There are physical responses, too. Living a mindful life strengthens the immune system, as well as our physiological responses to stress and negative emotions, boosts memory, increases the ability to focus, decreases our emotional reactivity, and encourages more cognitive flexibility. Our physical body is directly affected by our mental state, and being mindful keeps our bodies working more efficiently. Diet, exercise, and how we treat our body becomes more important by default when we are more aware of other aspects of our world. When we are becoming more in touch with ourselves, harming our bodies becomes something we don't want to enable. Nutritious food, healthy choices, and honoring our physique will happen more naturally as we work to become more mindful.

Practicing meditation can increase the benefits of being mindful. Meditative mindfulness practices have been shown to positively alter the structure and neural patterns in the brain, and strengthen the brain regions associated with heightened sensory processing and empathetic response. Therefore, people who regularly practice mindful meditation are literally rebuilding the structure of their brains to achieve desired outcomes. The mind is adaptable, so is the brain, and they go hand in hand.

Our relationships also improve, because mindfulness allows us to give and receive love more genuinely, as well as keep us from giving others power over our lives. Mindfulness brings us increased relationship satisfaction and strengthens morality and intuition. We feel more control over our own state of being, and gain confidence while moving through the world. It reduces stress and the stress hormone cortisol, assists in eliminating depression, and helps us to cope with anxiety. Living a life of mindfulness also increases good feelings such as well-being and happiness, increased openness to experiences, conscientiousness, and agreeableness.

It is believed that being mindful can improve self-control, objectivity, concentration, mental clarity, emotional maturity, the ability to better relate to others; as well as increase kindness, acceptance, and compassion. It's easy to see how this can be true once you've gotten to this point in the book. The process of getting to a place of mindfulness will give you all of these positive changes as you navigate through it.

CHAPTER 8

# HOW TO INCORPORATE MINDFULNESS INTO EVERYDAY TASKS

Mindfulness is the awareness of the present moment experienced without judgment. It has become more popular in recent years, moving from a largely obscure spiritual concept favored thousands of years ago, to the mainstream people of today. Anyone can benefit from being mindful.

In order to incorporate mindfulness into everyday tasks, you need only be aware, pay attention, and be present with no judgment. When performing everyday tasks, use your senses to perceive and process what you are doing, what is occurring around you. Look intently with your eyes, and really see what you are looking at. Examine it, notice the colors, the shapes, and decide whether you enjoy what you are seeing or not. What you do like, give your full attention, and feel the love you have for it. Watch the people and creatures around you. What do you find interesting? Is there more to learn? Enjoy yourself as you become a part of whatever is happening and embrace the things going on. Laugh, sing, move and use your body and mind. Listen carefully with your ears; hear all of the sounds around you. Notice how what you hear makes you feel, and if you need to eliminate the sounds that are overwhelming or bringing an annoying feeling. What are people saying to you? What are they communicating without words? How can you mindfully respond to them from a place of love? Smell what is there, and truly taste what you eat. Take note of the smells and tastes that you find appealing and allow yourself to be delighted by them. Feel the air on your skin, feel your feet on the ground, feel your heart beating in your chest, and remember to notice your breathing.

Just by giving your everyday tasks your full attention, and remaining present while doing them will put you in a position of being mindful. Everyone has things they have to do that don't feel glamorous or meaningful, and appreciating them anyway is how we keep our mind in the present. Humble thoughts, kind actions, and feeling grateful keep us mindful.

# CONCLUSION

Thank for making it through to the end of the *book*, let's hope it was informative and able to provide you with all of the tools you need to achieve your goals whatever it may be.

The hope is that this book has helped to bring you to a state of mindfulness, and confidence in knowing that you can return to that state again, and again. Mindfulness is an ongoing practice that one must remember to bring themselves back to using the tools given to them in this book. When we realize that mindfulness is simply paying attention without judgment, it is a lot easier said than done, unless we use the process laid out in this book to help guide us through it. In the world we live in, it is easy to get off track, but remembering to breathe can bring us back to center very quickly.

Using the things you learned in this book, you can now calmly acknowledge and accept your thoughts and feelings, and address them in an effort to keep them from holding you back. The words and actions of others will not interfere with your observation of the present moment because you can now impartially distance yourself from them, and realize that what others say and do has nothing to do with you, and everything to do with them. You can separate yourself from any situation and reflect on it objectively, free from judgment or resentment. Of course, none of us is perfect, and life can definitely make it difficult for mindfulness to come easily to you, and that is when you go back to the tools you learned in this book to help you get back on track.

Your life will feel differently now, in a much better way. You will notice more and will feel more compassionate and understanding toward others. You will become more aware of how very big our world is, and how small some of your problems can really be. What was once important to you may fall away. Things you decided were excess baggage in chapter five are no longer a part of your life, and there may be some fallout from that. Just remember to use what you have learned to counteract the effects of those casualties, and make room for more meaningful things to take your attention.

Now that you have learned the ins and outs of mindfulness, and the benefits it will bring you, it is your responsibility to share it with at least one person in order to help them and to help the world. The more popular mindfulness becomes, the more our world heals.

Finally, if you enjoyed this book, then I'd like to ask you for a favor, would you be kind enough to leave a review for this book on Amazon? It'd be greatly appreciated!

Thank you and good luck!

# EMPATH

*The Essential Guide to Understanding and Embracing*
*Your Gift While Using Meditation to Empower Yourself*

# INTRODUCTION

Congratulations on getting your personal copy of *Empath: The Essential Guide to Understanding and Embracing Your Gift While Using Meditation to Empower Yourself.*

## Are you an Empath?

An empath isn't defined by what they do, but what they are. If you're an empath, you were hard-wired to be that way since you were born and you have an ultimate purpose in this.

Most empaths don't realize that they can make a huge difference in the world by learning to let their special gift shine through and inspire others.

*The empath is like the cosmic, emotional cleaner.*

Their gift can be used to both service themselves and those around them, helping humankind transform into something freer.

## Working on Yourself as an Empath:

Essentially, what all empaths must do is some hard personal work. Since they are naturally focused on other people and caring for them, it can be difficult to do this.

*But learning to care for your gift, as an empath, is essential to making the most use of it.*

Focusing on this gives you the power to change your life and the world in a deep, meaningful way.

## Recognizing the Gift:

This book was written to help you realize that your nature is a blessing, not a curse. Once you recognize that, you will be able to lead a healthy and meaningful life.

*Negative lessons are what help us reach the positive, eventually.*

This is true for nearly all empaths. For most of them, the journey is tough and painful at first. For some reason, life for empaths often starts disempowered, and then they gain their true power later on.

The benefit of this is that they grow even stronger than they would have without this tough path. This strength will bring you closer to where you are meant to be.

Rest assured that if you're having a hard time with negativity in your life right now, you have the power to turn this around. You're on the start of your journey, and it's going to be worth all the effort at the end.

There are plenty of books on this subject on the market, thanks again for choosing this one! Every effort was made to ensure it is full of as much useful information as possible. Please enjoy!

# CHAPTER 1

# THE TRAITS AND PRICE
# OF HIGH EMPATHY

Are you a highly empathetic person (an empath)? How are you to know whether you are or not, for sure? The trait of high empathy happens in degrees. You can also cycle through different stages through life.

## Difficult Aspects of being an Empath:

If you fit into this category, it means you were put here for a purpose. Due to your nature, you have likely experienced some of the following challenges in life:

## Absorbing Negative Feelings:

Empaths pick up on energies around them, whether it's from people or objects. You might also pick up emotions from people who are not in your immediate vicinity.

## You feel the Weight of the World:

As an empath, you feel the weight of the world, and most of it doesn't even come from you. When others partake in negative behavior, it impacts you.

## You can Tell what people Think and Feel:

You pick up on people's feelings and thoughts and always want to help when they are undergoing something difficult. This can lead you into hard relationships with narcissists or other manipulative types.

## You get Taken Advantage of in Life:

You may have a hard time telling people no or standing up for yourself. For this reason, people often try to take advantage of you (and sometimes succeed).

## A Feeling of Personal Responsibility:

You have a feeling of personal responsibility towards those you care about and even those you don't, sometimes. If people don't appreciate your willingness to help, you may feel hurt.

## Surviving sensitivity:

Your next question is probably how can you survive this sensitivity? Our world has many selfish people in it and oftentimes, they come out on top. For people who have a big heart, this can be a challenge. You have likely already learned that, but this is only the beginning of working with that realization. Since you have already felt the bad aspects to this, it's your turn to find the light. You can get reacquainted with the positive aspects of your sensitivity, showing others that sensitivity and a loving nature can be the greatest asset.

## Why should you develop these Skills?

There are many advantages to developing your skills in empathy. A lot of empaths think that their sensitive nature has ruined any chance they may have had at happiness. They feel isolated and different from other people.

But there is a reason you're here and that is to embrace and love yourself, free from harsh judgments.

## The Challenges of the Path:

All over the internet, empaths talk about the challenges they endure. They might feel resentment toward others who haven't appreciated their gift and struggle as a result with low self-esteem. *You don't have to do this to yourself anymore.* Your ego, as everyone else's does, likes to create drama and negativity, but this is ignoring your real purpose on earth.

## Avoid the Blame game:

You should do whatever you can to avoid this pointless game of blaming others for your difficult path. Of course it's challenging to be this way, but you are closing yourself off to the benefits that come with it when you do this.

## Seeing the Purpose:

Think back to your past. If it weren't for your struggles in life, would you have found this book in the first place? You are meant to be reading this and you are meant to be where you are.

## The highest Spiritual Plane:

The empath is at the highest possible plane of spirituality that you can experience. Your nature has given you all of the tools you need to succeed and flourish in life.

## Empath Benefits:

Sometimes, you just need to be reminded of the benefits to your personality and nature. Here are some of the benefits to being highly empathetic:

## Intuitive Abilities:

Your abilities in intuition can go up to great heights extremely quickly as soon as you learn how to wield your empath powers in a healthy way. You are already naturally knowing and intuitive. This can skyrocket when you teach yourself to meditate and tap into something higher, which this book will cover.

## Abilities to Manifest:

As an empath, you are naturally great at manifesting your desires. Since you are already very aware of emotional vibration, you can use this to bring your desires to life.

## A Healing Nature:

Empaths are natural healers. These skills will get even better as you grow and let go of resentment and pain. As you heal other people, your self-healing will improve, as well.

## Tapping into Yourself:

Empaths have an easier time than most tapping into themselves because they can sense what they need through their own feelings. Your inner guidance system is naturally strong.

## Feeling the Emotions of the World:

An empath feels other people's feelings as if they are theirs. This includes pain and suffering of both friends and strangers. You may cry when you see a sad commercial or feel overcome with joy when you see others experience happiness.

## Naming your Nature:

You have probably known that you were different ever since childhood. But it's likely taken you a while to find the correct name to describe yourself. *Your nature is both good and bad.*

## Your Special Powers as an Empath:

Being an empath can give you awesome benefits as an artist, a leader, a marketer or a business owner. You can see into people's hearts and minds, understanding their aspirations and desires. When you can see straight into what someone truly cares about, both bad and good, you can cut straight to the chase, through confusing and distracting words.

## Connecting with the World:

Being an empath can also be a huge benefit for connecting with people when you interview them, present to them, or simply converse. You can feel your way through talks, getting right to what is most meaningful and relevant.

## Help with not Judging Others:

Being an empath can allow you to know what others are feeling and experiencing, seeing them from a place of non-judgment. This isn't always easy, of course. *But this comes at a tough cost...*

When you see someone hurting, you may get attached to and disturbed by this, whether they are a stranger to you or not. You may not even be able to help them if you are too strongly affected.

## Business Challenges for the Empath:

As a professional, the tough side of empathy comes up when you want to know how to serve clients or customers. Translating this to money, brands, and businesses ca be hard.

Separating yourself from emotion in a professional situation can be the hardest part of your career. So what can you do about this difficulty? Should you disconnect from the world? Be as shielded as you can? Or hide behind sarcasm and humor?

## The Ultimate Goal- Acceptance:

It's a big enough challenge to deal with your own feelings, let alone the feelings of everyone else around you. But once you see into what it means to be an empath, you will accept it with open arms. Because feeling is what it means to be truly alive. It's what connects is with each other, fueling experience and interaction.

## Navigating Challenging Situations:

The difficult part is always to figure out when you should let the flood of emotion in, or when to shield yourself from it. And how to let enough in to help others without harming yourself. You've probably already been trying to figure this out for years. Most empaths struggle plenty before reaching any sort of clarity.

## The Connection with Art and Empathy:

Many empaths seek refuge in creation and many of the greatest writers and artists in the world had a highly empathetic nature. This is often a matter of survival rather than just a mere hobby.

## The Role of Mindfulness:

Many empaths will find empowerment in a simple concept, which we will talk about throughout this book; mindfulness. This won't make all of your struggles magically disappear. But it will allow you to figure out what you're drawing to you and then choose how to use your compassion and empathy in the appropriate way.

## More Challenges of High Empathy:

If you have already figured out that you're an empath, you're aware of the struggles that come along with it. You feel the world and emotions very deeply. You also require a lot of solitary time to process these feelings.

Empaths can also get hurt very easily in relationships. Thankfully, there's a way to make this path easier and more fulfilling for you. But first, let's look deeper into some of the empath challenges.

## Getting Overwhelmed by Crowds:

Empaths often feel very uncomfortable in noisy and crowded places. You may instantly shrink away from areas full of chaos and move toward relaxing, calm environments. But to many empaths, a lot of places seem loud and hectic, especially cities. This presents a huge problem for you. In one way, you enjoy solitude and quiet more than most, but this can lead you into isolation.

Empaths might not have a lot of friends because of this trait and build shells around themselves to protect their sensitive nature.

## Empaths are Great Lovers and Friends:

Regardless of their sensitivity and avoidance of harsh social environments, you will never have a better lover or friend than an empath. Finding those you connect well with, however, is the hard part.

## Your Tendency to get hurt:

Empaths are open books which means that they might get hurt very easily. This vulnerable tendency can draw those to them who want to take advantage of them. For this reason, their relationship history might be difficult.

## High Running Emotions:

Empaths are individuals with beautiful and sensitive hearts, meaning that they have high running emotions. This can lead other people to feel like they need to walk on eggshells around the empath. You may retreat into nature to get some time alone because you feel isolated from the rest of the world.

## You get told to be Less Sensitive:

Perhaps one of the most hurtful thing to an empath is being told that they should stop being so sensitive. You have likely heard that you need to grow up and be less emotional many times in your life. These heartless statements can really hurt. Some are just built more sensitive than other people, but not everyone realizes this. Empaths will never tell others to have a thinner skin, so getting told to develop a thicker one can hurt.

## Emotional Imbalance:

As an empath, you often feel emotionally imbalanced. In fact, this may even be the norm for you. Empaths have higher rates of depression and anxiety because they live with their hearts instead of their minds. Their emotions take control and they often feel dragged around by them. When it comes to large crowds or people, empaths might get overwhelmed and imbalanced. This can lead to panic attacks in severe situations.

Since you take on the feelings of others all the time, you are getting bombarded with countless different emotional signals at any given time. This leads you to get drained quickly and understandably so. *Feeling so much all the time is exhausting.*

## Good-Natured but Bad Advice:

One tiny event can send your emotions into a severe downward spiral that is rarely, if ever, understood by your friends and family. They might even tell you to stop thinking so much. However, this advice is worthless to you, regardless of how well-meaning it is. You can't simply shut off what you feel and shouldn't have to.

## The Risk of Bad Habits:

As an empath, you live on your feelings and at times, you feel like you can only handle them by picking up unhealthy addictions and bad habits. Here are some examples of those:

- **Drugs:** Drugs can be a huge distraction from your feelings, deadening you to them and making the emotional signals more bearable, at least temporarily.

- **Food:** Many empaths retreat into eating to distract themselves from their own anxiety, depression, and pain.

- **Other People:** Relationships or even friendships can also be used as an avenue to suppress your feelings and avoid dealing with them. But these relationships will always end badly.

## You Might be at Risk:

As a highly sensitive empath, you don't know how to deal with the turbulence going on inside you and look to external sources for healing. Even those who engage in meditation and healthy habits are at risk for becoming addicted to something harmful because of this. So make sure that you are aware of this and exercise caution at all times.

# CHAPTER 2

# UNDERSTANDING THE GIFT

Empaths can, and do, soak up the emotions and thoughts of other people, taking them on as their own. Toy don't empathize in the way that others do, by imagining how someone feels. Rather, they literally feel it as their own emotion. This is one of the many things that separates the empath from most other people and why they can be hard to understand.

## The Necessity of Proper Development:

It's no secret to you that this ability is quite a nightmare at times. But to avoid this, you need to learn how to develop it properly. When you take on others' feelings, day in and day out, you become covered with chaotic energy that can weigh you down, leading to fear, anxiety, and despair. In severe cases, empaths may even become suicidal. *But it doesn't have to be this way.*

## The Mastery of Empathy:

It's possible to master your art and gift of empathy. You can get to the point where when you are with other people, you can feel deeply into what they are going through.

## Going Deeper into Emotional Blocks:

Let's again go over some of the advantages and benefits of the highly empathetic nature. In order to truly get rid of the distortion around your power, you have to first sense the truth hidden within it. You are activating this difficult state because you are holding yourself back and feeling hopeless. The answer is to feel into the blockages.

## Harmonizing with Others:

When you embrace your empathetic abilities as a catalyst for spiritual experience, this means you can harmonize and feel into other people's emotions. Next, acting as their catalyst, you can bring energy and attention to their blockages. You can direct their focus to the most important areas, allowing them to feel them in a new way.

## Using Questions:

You can utilize questioning to find out why they have a blockage. This can lead to a beautiful release of pent up emotion in the other person.

## Alchemical Transformation and Healing:

When you feel as though you're reaching to the depth of that person, harmonizing, this blockage will fall away on its own as their soul is reminded of itself. Then they can integrate this work and alchemical healing can occur in them.

## The Necessity of Empathetic Abilities:

None of the above could even happen without the qualities of high empathy. But the empath is more than just a catalyst for these experiences. They accept the details and nuances of other's emotions. This gift can bring about unseen powers in the other, those which are hidden and repressed.

This is why the gift of the empath matters so much for the world. They should be cherished and appreciated, rather than seen as flawed in some way.

## The Importance of Personal Boundaries:

Before an empath's skills are developed, they will feel like a huge affliction and struggle. How can you handle this problem? Setting appropriate boundaries is a good place to begin.

## Getting to Know yourself:

The first step means recognizing what your own inner calm and peace feels like; begin able to sense your vibration no matter what situation you're in. You need to explore yourself and your own vibes as often as you can in order to learn how to see it, especially during challenging times.

## Finding your Own Peace:

Once you get to know your own vibration, you will be able to find it, no matter what you're surrounded by. This means finding your own practices and rituals, such as meditation and yoga. It also means paying attention to health, what you eat, and the habits you engage in (as mentioned earlier).

## Noticing what serves you:

Since you are a highly sensitive person, you need to focus on what serves you to find your vibration. Anything else means compromising your deepest self.

## Resisting being the Diplomat:

The empath has a naturally diplomatic sense of being. They wish to connect, harmonize, and bring joy to others. But this can get tricky when they stretch their own boundaries to help others at their own peril.

## Closing down isn't Necessary:

You need to embrace the fact that you can serve as a catalyst for other people and resist the urge to close yourself off to the outside world. All you need to do is set clear boundaries.

## To set Boundaries, you must know them:

You can only start to affect the world positively when you are aware of your boundaries. This will help you stay clear in your purpose, increasingly calm and centered instead of tossed about by chaotic feelings constantly. Once you experience some negative emotions coming at you, how can you work with this?

Assess your internal state, take some deep breaths, and release the negative feelings. You can breathe in, consciously relaxing, holding your breath in and filling it with light, and then exhaling.

## Acceptance and True Release:

When you do this, you are saying yes to the energy and accepting it, allowing it to enter you, but also accepting that the energy is not you. You can positively impact this with your awareness before you exhale it.

## This is not Rejection of your Gift:

Keep in mind that doing this does not mean rejecting your gift at all. It just involves refusing to get lost in it to your own detriment. This means you can have a positive impact on the world by asserting your power, first to yourself, then to those around you.

## This takes Practice:

There are going to be times where the energy coming into you gets stuck. This is because you aren't used to releasing it in this way and habit can be strong. At this time, you need to check the following:

- **Are you judging yourself?** When you judge yourself for the reactions you have to a strong emotion, you are stemming the flow and blocking yourself off. Start to notice when you do this.

- **Have you tried Surrendering?** You need to first recognize your own judgements and then work with them by being easier on yourself. Keep in mind that accepting the feelings doesn't mean agreeing to hold onto them. Bringing light into these difficult feelings will enable you to release them and feel a great sense of inner peace.

So learn to feel your own resistance, soften into it, let them unwind, meld yourself to them, and then allow yourself to let them go.

## Committing to Continuous Development:

An empath must continuously develop their gift. Remember to see the deeper spiritual catalyst in your skill and be proud of what you can offer. You are here for a reason!

## Mastery is Possible:

Hopefully, these tools will allow you to integrate and ease into your gift. You can master it and improve the world in the hardest of times.

## Don't downplay yourself:

People everywhere are finally waking up to their empathetic nature but don't know how to handle it or control it. Those of you reading this book likely know this struggle well. Many empaths are confused about what is happening inside of them, feeling everything around them so deeply that they feel knocked around by their emotions.

It can be tempting, when you're an empath, to just call yourself too emotional or even unbalanced. But thankfully, you don't have to downplay your gift. You can use your skill to your benefit.

## Feelings- Your Greatest Tool:

To start to understand the war of emotions going on inside you all the time, you have to first accept that your emotions are your biggest power. They are your guidance, greatest tool, and your closest friend, not your enemy.

## So where do you start to understand this?

1. Figure out where the feeling is arising from. Every time you feel something strong or overwhelming, find out whether it's really yours or not. Your intuition already knows the answer.

2. Welcome the feeling. If the feeling you are feeling is yours, try to welcome it. Let yourself the same empathy you give to others. Feel the emotion completely and let yourself know it's alright.

3. Envision that you are seeing the feeling from your highest sense of perspective, like you're not in your own body. Try to view your feelings from outside.

4. Find the belief that is at the core of the emotion so you can soothe and validate it. Find out what the belief is behind your feeling. What thoughts are going through your mind that are leading to this emotional reaction?

5.  Where is the emotion lodged in your body? Most of us can sense some kind of tension in our bodies when we feel negative emotions, such as our neck, hips, or throat.

6.  Switch the object of your focus willingly. Once you have soothed and validated your strong emotion, attempt to find some thoughts that will lift your mood up. Find anything that will make you feel happier than you were before, even slightly.

7.  Don't ignore your feelings. The idea is to change your focus, not to reject what your emotions are. Recognize the feeling, validate it, and send it positive energy.

8.  Transform the feeling. Once you recognize the negative feeling, you can transform it into something else. Imagine that you are allowing the emotion to pass through your body and change into something else.

By doing this, you can become an alchemist of feelings. Envision the feeling, such as sadness, being changed into happiness, and then beam it out of your body into the outside world.

This is much easier when you are transmuting someone else's feelings, because you already recognize that they are not really you. Try doing this with yourself by realizing that even your own emotions don't have to get stuck inside of you.

## Using Visualization:

Many empaths will find that visualization is a powerful tool for healing themselves and working with their special gift. For many of them, the more they visualize, the biter they will feel. When you start to shield, try to use your visualization abilities. What is that allows you to feel truly peaceful and joyful?

Which colors do you associate with pure peace? How do you want to heal other people's energies and emotions using your power? You can envision your shield being infused with every powerful intention you have. Since you are related to and entangled with everyone you relate to personally, you will notice that you can lift heavy emotions at will.

Each time you send out this transformed emotional energy back into the world, the other person will feel lighter.

## Embracing your Empathetic Personality:

You must recognize that your empathy is your way to give back to the earth. This is how you can heal others. Your skill should be embraced, not feared or rejected.

## Putting up a Shield in Public:

When you are very sensitive and empathetic, you should put up a shield every time you go into crowded or public areas. This doesn't have to be done out of fear, but instead can be done out of self-love and love for other people.

## Being Brave enough to Stop Hiding:

Shielding isn't about hiding your skill from the world, but about learning how to use it in a manner that helps the world and yourself. Learning how to soothe yourself will help you notice emotions bouncing off your protective shield.

## An Automated Process:

This will eventually become an automated process, especially if you infuse your shield with specific intentions to stay positive and comfortable. Eventually, this becomes your natural state of being.

## Have you Tried Everything?

Many empaths feel as though they have already tried everything possible to become healthier and more balanced, to no avail. If you feel this way, but still struggle with controlling your skills, it may help you to reach out to an empath community online. *Here are some of the benefits of doing this:*

## Power in Connection:

When you can relate to others who are also empaths, you feel validated. You no longer have to wonder if you're inventing your personality or making it up.

## Being able to Vent:

You will finally be able to vent to people who understand you and will be able to offer you words of wisdom. Empaths need empathy too. Everyone needs support sometimes, so don't hold back on asking for help or support if you feel like you could use it.

# CHAPTER 3

# ARE YOU AN EMPATH?

Empathy means being able to understand and read other people's emotions, either involuntarily or voluntarily. Empaths can scan the feelings and thoughts of another person to find out where they are mentally and emotionally. Even though this is normal for them, empaths rarely understand the way this works or why it does. But they always realize that they are more sensitive, usually from a young age.

## Telltale Signs of being an Empath:

If you still aren't certain of whether you fall into this category or not, looking over this list can help you decide and act accordingly.

## You sense deep Emotions:

Empathy means feeling someone else's feeling and relating to them through this. It means being able to look beyond the surface to see the genuine emotion beneath the façade people put up. You can sense what is going on behind the mask and extend compassionate help to the other, allowing them to feel more comfortable with their own thoughts.

## You have a sense of Intuitive Knowing:

Empaths are extremely sensitive people. Sensitivity is a word used to describe someone's ability to sense other people's feelings and emotions. Empaths feel an intuitive knowing that often comes along with understanding, consideration, and compassion for all living things.

## Various Strength Levels:

With empathy comes varying strength levels which come from the person's self-awareness and understanding of their skill. This also has to do with how much they accept their nature. Most empaths don't learn about what their personality really means until they are older and have already struggled to find the answer for many years.

## Who do Empaths Empathize with?

In short, everyone. Empaths will feel empathy toward their friends, children, family, strangers, animals, and even objects or plants. Empathy goes beyond space and time. For this reason, empaths can even feel others' emotions from far away. Some relate more to animals, others relate more to humans, and some are a mix.

## Is this Trait Inherited?

Some believe that empathy is a genetic quality that comes along with our DNA, passed down from our parents. This phenomenon in human psychology is studied by both new age health practitioners and traditional science.

## A Spiritual and Genetic Quality:

Empathy is both genetic and spiritual in nature. Empaths can sense other people on more than just one level. As they observe what others think, feel, and say, they see beyond what others do. They can get extremely proficient with interpreting other people's nonverbal signals or the tiny expressions of their face. Although this isn't empathy, it is related.

## The Mechanics of Empathy:

How exactly does empathy work? Although plenty exists that we don't understand yet on this topic, people have discovered some key information. Everything on earth has a frequency or vibration and empaths can pick up on these and notice when even the smallest shifts occur in them.

## Vocal Expressions:

Expressive words have within them a pattern of energy that comes from the person speaking them. They hold a particular meaning that is specific to the one speaking the words. Within this expression is a force field or power, also called energy. For instance, words like "hate" immediately call to mind an intense emotion, strengthened by the speaker's emotion.

The energy behind the word is what the empath senses, even if the word is not spoken. The empath will sense the emotion even if the thought is only there without bodily or verbal expression.

## Who is the Empath?

An empath can be compared to a moving poet. They are almost always creative in some way, skilled in imagination, and gifted artists, singers, or writers. They are humorous and loyal, with a broad perspective towards the world. The empath is a doctor, teacher, nurse, friend, father, and mother. They also make skilled healers and clairvoyants, though not always. In other words, an empath can take just about any form and they exist everywhere in the world.

## The Most Skilled Listeners:

If there's one talent an empath has (in addition to their tendency toward creativity), it's listening. They are affectionate both in words and personality, great with counseling and listening, both with friends and strangers.

They often help people to the point of putting themselves second. They can also be withdrawn, closed off from the world, neurotic, and lonely, depending on how they express, accept, or reject their gift of heightened empathy.

## Animal and Nature Lovers:

Empaths are very passionate about nature and have a deep respect for it. Empaths enjoy walking, beaches, water, the outdoors, and especially animals. They find their way outside whenever they need time away to reflect.

This is their chance to bring clarity back to their senses and find peace within themselves. This act of retreat into nature becomes essential to the empath's peace of mind.

## The Qualities of the Empath:

Empaths can be very quiet and might have trouble accepting compliments since they prefer to say kind things about other people. They are very expressive friends and don't hesitate to share personal information about themselves.

## Trouble Expressing Strong Emotion:

Despite the fact that they are open about themselves, they might not have the easiest time putting words to their intense feelings.

## Blocking out Other People:

In addition to being open, an empath can also be unresponsive and aloof to those around them. When they need to, some of them can be good at ignoring other people.

## More in touch with the Outside than the Inside:

Some empaths find it easier to feel and sense what is in the external world, rather than the internal world. This can lead them to disregard their personal needs.

## The Peacemaking Empath:

Typically, empaths are non-aggressive, non-violent, and like to make peace between people arguing. When they are in a situation with disharmony, they feel extremely uncomfortable.

## Avoiding Confrontation:

In the rare case that the empath ends up in a confrontational situation, they will do everything they can to fix it. When they speak out of anger, they immediately regret it and try to fix the situation.

## Sensitivity to a lot of Stimuli:

Most empaths are not only sensitive to feelings, but also to the news, movies, videos, and TV. Emotional drama or violence in movies, especially concerning violence toward animals or children, can make the empath cry or feel sick to their stomach.

They will often puzzle over how humans could be so cruel and have a hard time expressing their feelings when someone doesn't show compassion. Even if they try, justifying cruelty is impossible for them.

## People are drawn to Empaths:

Many people are drawn to empaths. Even when others don't know why, they are pulled toward them and want to be around them as much as possible. The empathetic personality is very warm and magnetic to both people and animals. Even strangers may find themselves sharing personal information with empaths. They probably understand, on some intuitive level, that the empath will understand.

## Great Problem Solvers:

In addition to their great listening skills and impressive creativity, empaths are also great studiers, thinkers, and problem solvers. If they see a problem, they want to fix it.

CHAPTER 4

# SHIELDING YOURSELF FROM HARM

Some research has supported the idea that highly sensitive people could have a constantly activated amygdala. This part of the brain is a cluster of nuclei, shaped like an almond and located deep in your brain. This crucial cluster plays an important role in the processing of your emotions. When emotion is aggressive, your amygdala is extra active. The triggering of this cluster sets off stress hormones in your body.

## Empaths and the Amygdala:

Studies have shown that when highly sensitive people saw photos of suffering, this activated their amygdala. This led to the release of adrenaline and cortisol, further fueling an intense emotional response.

## The Amygdala doesn't think:

This part of the brain does not reason, but only reacts. When fear, strong emotion, or stress becomes activated, the fight or flight reaction gets kicked into gear. This response is our body's mechanism for keeping us free from dangerous events and elevates our hormones to allow us the strength and energy to escape harm.

## What do these Hormones do?

Cortisol and adrenalin, the stress hormones that the amygdala activation releases into your body increase your glucose levels, respiration, and heart rate. All of this is meant to induce physical activity. When your body is constantly being exposed to these hormones, your organs become knocked out of balance. This can lead to issues like diabetes, adrenal fatigue, and heart disease.

## The Empath's Reaction to Pain:

The empath doesn't have to see someone experiencing suffering or enduring pain, just being around them can cause a reaction, even when that person is trying to hide their true emotions. This can lead to an overproduction of cortisol and adrenalin.

## Possible Health Issues for the Empath:

In typical situations, once the stress trigger is gone, levels of stress go back to their normal state and the amygdala is no longer active. But when these triggers don't go away, issues come up, which is where the empath may be in trouble. Empaths can't escape overwhelming emotions very easily. They have to not only take on their own feelings and stress, but other people's stress.

Empaths might cease feeling these external emotions after they leave the vicinity, but not always. Some vibrations can cling to their psyche for days, activating the amygdala and causing more stress hormones to be released.

## What can be done about this?

The next logical question to be asked is what the solution is for this problem. Let's go over some steps you can take to prevent unnecessary stress in your life.

## Stay away from Triggers:

The most important step you can take is to stay away from stress triggers whenever possible. If you know anyone who makes you feel a negative reaction for an extended period (like multiple hours or a full day), stay away from them. The amygdala isn't only activated by present situations, but can also become activated while you think about difficult or emotional memories. If there's someone in your life who brings you pain and suffering, do yourself a favor and disengage.

## Be in Control of your Thoughts:

Keeping your mind as silent as possible is your best defense against emotional stress triggers. There are a few methods for this, such as visiting nature on a regular basis and meditation, which we will cover later on in the book.

## Get Enough Exercise:

The best remedy for stress is exercise. It can help your body clear out extra stress hormones, helping prevent the damage that occurs from too much.

## Stay away from Caffeine:

Sensitive people react more strongly to coffee and other types of stimulants than others. Sugar can also be a trigger for unnecessary stress, so be mindful of your diet. Be sure to drink plenty of water and eat fresh, whole foods whenever you can. Some empaths carry around extra fat on their belly, which is a signal that your body is taking in too much sugar or sugar forming foods. If this applies to you, it's a sure sign that you are out of balance.

## The Importance of Staying Grounded:

These days, everyone is being bombarded with negative energy. This is a challenge for most, but it hits the empath especially hard. Even if you stay at home in your personal space, your antenna might be picking up disturbing stimuli and throwing your mood off. Due to this, you may feel drained and distracted a lot of the time.

## Protecting yourself:

In order to fight against this perpetually overwhelmed and exhausted state, you have to both stay grounded and learn how to protect yourself from harm.

## The Best Tips for staying Grounded:

All people are different, so you have to look and try methods until you find the right one for you. But most find that the most effective way to keep yourself grounded is to have a healthy, resilient body, a silent mind, and a centered field of energy. Here are some steps for achieving just that.

## Getting plenty of Water:

Our bodies are 75 percent water, so it's not surprising that it's high on the scale for self-healing. A lot of people don't realize that they are very dehydrated. Not getting enough water makes you age faster and impacts your mental state. Water has an extremely calming effect on empaths and they have to get plenty, both outside and inside of them.

Most empaths should try to drink pure water and get a lot of it. The more you weigh, the more you need to drink. Water not only clears away the dirt from your body but can help clear away negative energies. If you don't believe this, next time you get off work and feel stressed out, try to take a shower instead of pouring a glass of wine and notice how it clears and uplifts your mind. You can also drink a glass of cold water to reduce the impact of negative emotions.

## Grounding Foods:

Another crucial method for being more grounded in your life is eating grounding foods instead of drug-like food. Sugar and wheat have a negative impact on all bodies, but the empath is especially susceptible to their bad effects.

People that are very sensitive can pick up on energy vibrations. Everything on earth vibrates at various frequencies, even alcohol, drugs, and food. Empaths have a hugely negative reaction to anything that has a bad or low vibration. Most alcohol and drugs have this, bringing you down very quickly. Even though some foods are not classed as drugs, they have a similarly negative effect on your body.

If you have a hard time maintaining balance and staying grounded, even when you think often about the subject of self-help and growth, look at your diet. Even those who practice meditation, yoga, and positivity will have a hard time if they have a bad diet.

## Using Sea Salt:

It's believed that Hippocrates, the father of medicine, discovered that sea salt has amazing healing abilities. Sea salt is both a healer and a purifier, with the power to dissolve and draw out negative energies from our physical and emotional bodies. This is useful for empaths who need to interact with others a lot and pick up on their anxious or stressed out energies. Salt can not only ground you but clear energies from your home.

## Balance out your Vibe and energy:

By making sure your masculine and feminine parts are balanced with each other, you will stay balanced. This means making sure you are paying attention to your soft, emotional side just as much as your logical, assertive side.

There are countless ways to get in touch with both of these sides of you and all of us have both within us. You can do some extra research on this subject if you feel as though either your masculine or feminine energies are out of balance.

## Smudging your Home:

Smudging with a bundle of sage can help clear out negative or unwanted energies from your home. This is especially important if an argument or confrontation has occurred in it in recent times.

## Get Toned:

In the modern world, many people start exercising so they can lose weight or get toned. It does offer a lot more than this, but a strong body makes you stronger emotionally, as well. Exercise releases toxins, energizes you, uplifts your mood, and makes you happier. It's also very powerful for grounding you in difficult times.

You can find an exercise that you actually enjoy. It doesn't have to be a chore. If you dislike set times, routines, or rules, you can make your own rules and go freestyle with your exercise routine. You can jog, dance, run, or do whatever it is that appeals most to you for working up a sweat and getting active.

## Being Creative:

In our modern world full of routine and rules, we hardly have time to get creative. Creativity adds to feeling good, and feeling good keeps you grounded. Genuine creation from your interests and passion will uplift your psyche and keep dark feelings and thoughts at bay. As you can see, this is an invaluable activity for empaths to engage in.

## Balancing the Chakras:

We all have seven chakras, which make up our body of energy. These are the spiritual power centers that go up your body, starting from the base of your spine and extending to your head. Chakras, which are aligned with our endocrine system, are constantly whirling and moving. Any time one of them is thrown off balance, we feel it inside.

Empaths are especially sensitive to this reaction, so figuring out ways to balance it will aid you in staying grounded and provide you with amazing health benefits. We will discuss more on the chakras in chapter eight of this book.

## Practicing Yoga:

A lot of people think that yoga isn't their thing, but it just might be the ones who think this that could benefit most from it. Yoga is very grounding for empaths and works on both the energetic and physical bodies.

Yoga helps create a flexible, mobile spine, which is related to youthfulness, but yoga is built upon breathing. As you breathe consciously, it will calm and still your mind while strengthening the body. Regardless of your flexibility or age, yoga can benefit you. Start by looking up some poses online and finding something easy to start with.

## Meditation and the Empath:

Meditation is an important tool for the empath, especially when you are busy and have a head full of fearful thoughts and chatter. As most empaths do, you likely have a chaotic mind. Meditation will aid you in dealing with stress, providing you with clear insights. We will discuss some more details on meditation in chapter seven of this book.

## Seeking Refuge in Nature:

As mentioned before, being outdoors can ground and heal the empath immediately. If you have a job that keeps you inside most of the time, or live in a crowded city, you will have a hard time finding balance or staying grounded. Here are some tips for making sure you get enough nature.

## Taking Weekend Trips:

When you don't live near a park, you should make sure you are taking regular trips on the weekends to see some nature and escape the smog.

## Have Plants inside:

If you have to work inside and feel disconnected from nature, having some plants in your home is better than nothing.

## Making Time for Humor in your Life:

As adults, we are pressured to be serious and solemn, and don't have enough time to have fun. When is the last time you laughed for real? Kids laugh constantly because they haven't yet learned how to be serious in life. They stay grounded because they always play.

## Spend Time with Kids:

You can learn a lot from children, in this way. Try to keep your inner child alive and well by seeking out fun and play. This is very therapeutic for the spirit and you will notice the difference.

## Watch Funny Movies:

Humor is good for the soul and relieving stress. Try to prioritize watching comedy movies at least once a week so you can have a good laugh.

## Using Crystals:

Some people find relief in healing crystals. Cultures such as ancient Egypt and Atlantis have long recognized their healing power. Some believe that they can heal physical, mental, and emotional blockages.

Crystals may be used for chakra healing to both remove blockages and balance the chakras. Due to their natural vibrations of healing, a lot of empaths are drawn to these stones for their protective and grounding abilities.

## Using Essential Oils:

Similar to crystals, essential oils also have healing properties that empaths may be drawn to. Essential oil benefits can be obtained through scent or through topical application with a carrier oil (such as olive oil or almond oil).

- **Calming Oils:** Oils such as lavender, ylang-ylang, and vanilla have a calming effect on the senses and can be used to soothe anxiety and help induce sleep.

- **Invigorating Oils:** Empaths often get worn out from carrying the weight of everyone's emotions every day. Oils such as cinnamon or citrus oils can help you feel energized and invigorated again.

## Walking Barefoot Outside:

A lot of people underestimate the value of walking without shoes. This can help you become grounded instantly. This will help you feel more connected to the earth and grounded in reality, so try to do it regularly.

## In Conclusion:

There you have the best grounding techniques for empaths. I hope that this chapter helped you in understanding the way your habits affect your wellbeing and emotional health.

# CHAPTER 5

# STOP TAKING ON THE BURDENS OF OTHERS

It's obvious to every empath that life is a challenge sometimes, especially for you, who feels very deeply and is strongly impacted by everyone else's energies and moods. But rather than seeking comfort in bad addictions such as binge-watching television, drinking, or eating unhealthy food, you can do an easy, simple meditation and re-center yourself at will. Here are some of the most common empath triggers that cause stress, and some easy practices you can put to use to help keep the stress at a minimum.

## If you are having Junk Food Cravings...

Next time you're stressed out and overwhelmed in relation to the emotions you're picking up, as well as your own reaction to them, and get the urge to binge eat, try this. Sit at your pantry or fridge and attempt to feel what is going on beneath the craving. Is it excitement, sadness, loneliness, or just plain old stress?

Even just leaving a note on your refrigerator that states your intention to eat healthier and be more conscious, that can be enough instead of sitting.

## When you're dealing with a Narcissist:

This is another challenging situation that every empath has dealt with before, on some level. Next time this happens to you, excuse yourself to go outside or near a window.

## Conscious Breathing:

Then you should slow your breath down with your eyes closed, breathing in as deeply as you can. Imagine someone or something you really love, like the ocean or your child. This will allow you to feel centered and feel from your heart space. This will also allow you to manage and deal with the energy of the person stressing you out.

## Remind yourself that you can't Change anyone...

Empaths want to heal people and make them feel better. But every once in a while, you have to remind yourself that you can't heal or help everyone. Some people, you must send them your blessing (internally) and let them go.

## When your Colleague's Mood is Contagious:

This is the best time to put up your visual shield to protect against the vibes around you. Otherwise, they can pull you down into a bad mood. You can use your centering techniques from the previous chapter for keeping yourself in a good state of mind. This will help no matter who is stressing you out.

# CHAPTER 6

# THE EMPATH'S PURPOSE

One very common asked question of empaths is what their purpose really is on this earth. This question can feel painful to carry around and seemingly find no answers. The empath finds this common question all the more troubling because they have a skill and gift that others don't understand, and on top of that, they have no clue how to use it in the right way.

## How can you help?

Empaths often wonder how they can service others or help them in a real, deep way. It's a normal trait for most empaths to wish to help people, particularly when they are in pain. But empaths have often tried and not been able to help people reach deeper into themselves and find their own answers. For the empath, it's crushing to witness this pain and be powerless to stop it.

## Suffering is not All Bad:

Suffering is what allows humans to evolve, find a clearer path, and awaken to their truest selves. Suffering also allows people to reach a more spiritual lifestyle and state of being.

## Suffering is not Knowing Purpose:

A lot of people feel as though they are experiencing pain when they are disconnected from what their purpose is. Every person needs purpose and direction in life, regardless of how much they have evolved and grown in the past. It's up to every individual to find their own direction and question their life.

## Working with Others:

Some empaths feel like their truest purpose is to work with and serve others through healing. Some have this gift but would rather be more solitary in their lives. Neither of these is wrong, but it's highly personal. This means that only you can decide what your purpose is in life.

## Working more indirectly:

You don't have to work with people closely to serve and heal them. As an empath, you already help other people more than they or you realize. People transform negative energy, often without knowing they are doing it. And as they take this on, transforming the energy, they are servicing the world.

## Great at Listening:

In addition, empaths are good at listening, as mentioned before. At times, listening to someone can be a healing experience in itself, unless you're dealing with a narcissist.

## Most don't listen:

People hardly ever listen and most are busy talking or thinking about themselves. Empaths, on the other hand, do listen and can hear on a deeper wavelength. In addition, they care about what they're hearing.

## You DO Help:

Empaths can heal in many other ways, too. So if you think you aren't actually helping anyone, think again, because you are!

## Improving the World:

If you are working on improving yourself, you are improving the world, which is the best thing you can do for yourself. In summary, you can find your ultimate purpose by nurturing your spirit, body, and mind.

If you're true to yourself and stick with your interests and passions, everything else will fall into place. If you are following and loving everything you do, happiness will come to you. *And happiness is how you find your purpose.*

## You're already on the Path:

Whether you realize it or not, you're following your path, though you don't always notice it. The troubles you've gone through and beat are part of the path. Reading this book is related to your destiny since you had to take certain steps and have certain experiences to make it here. Reading this book was meant to be, for you. Even when you aren't completely ready, you can plant seeds and use the information you need.

## You were born this Way for a Purpose:

You are sensitive like this for a good reason. You aren't being punished. This is a way to become more emotionally strong and understand and help the world. Your intuition, empathy, and strong feelings all make up a difficult road to travel. This road is full of countless lows and highs and the experiences you have are worth a world of pain and emotions.

You feel not only your own emotions, but others, and as a result, have a special insight into humanity and the world around you. You are learning constantly, even if you don't realize it at the time.

## Seeing Root Causes:

As soon as you gain an awareness of what is causing your imbalance, and overcome it, you will be free to truly pursue the life you wish to live. As soon as you are done with this book, you'll see your insecurities for what they are.

## Self-Healing:

As soon as you recognize your insecurities, you will know what you have to do to truly heal. Once you take this path, your real purpose will become real.

## A Normal Struggle to have:

A lot of people struggle to find their purpose, it isn't only empaths. In our fast-changing world, people are becoming increasingly lost. Empaths often feel confused about whether they are following the correct path for their career or not. Even if they have a job they like, they may feel a deeper purpose pulling them in another direction.

Countless reasons exist for that, but how strongly impacted they are by emotions is one reason why they are confused in this way. Since the empath will get physically and emotionally exhausted in the world, they may just feel unfulfilled. They then tend to blame this on their life circumstances or career, even if that has nothing to do with it. Having low vitality can keep you disconnected from your intuition and true direction.

### Absorbing Energy:

When you are always absorbing the emotional energy of other people, you are going to feel drained. Being drained means that no matter what job you have, you'll feel fed up.

### Exhaustion:

Since they are exhausted and fed up, they start to question the job they have. Regardless of the situation, empaths will become drained and exhausted when they get overstimulated.

### Non-negative Stimulation:

When an empath gets overwhelmed, it isn't always from bad energies. Even nervousness, exhilaration, or excitement can cause them to feel too much adrenaline and get burned out. If you work somewhere surrounded by nervous energy or excitement, this can also cause you to get overwhelmed. Empaths often find being around kids very tiring for this reason.

### Destructive Energies:

Being around negative energy or highly charged situations can be bad for you as you get weighed down by the low frequency vibrations. You will become not only weighed down, but drained eventually. Although empaths may be drawn to medical professions, such as nursing, they may find it hard to handle over time due to all the anxious energy present in their world.

Since empaths are nurturing and caring, they feel compelled to help the suffering of the world. They might wish to have a service job for that reason. But this type of job can end up making them exhausted, especially once they are over 30.

## The Necessity of Grounding and Empowering:

This is why empowering and grounding techniques matter so much. People who aren't empaths don't get how easily they can become exhausted. Rather, others may accuse them of not caring, being lazy, or avoiding responsibility.

## Struggling with Confidence:

When an empath is seeking a new job, a low sense of self-esteem can hold you back from really trying to go for what you want. If they don't see why they feel this way, they should try to see if maybe they are picking up someone else's insecurity and taking it on as their own.

## Paying Attention to your Company:

If you are around people too often who aren't confident in themselves, you will eventually soak up this. Figuring out which emotions are yours and which are not is what you have to do to balance yourself. This won't happen overnight and there are countless layers to this. This will be a painful and difficult process, but very worth it. If you are desiring to grow in your empath abilities, it's going to take effort and lots of work from you, but you'll start noticing changes and it will be worth it.

## The Blissful Empath Life:

You might be skeptical about this, but it's possible to live a blissful life. Living your purpose and waiting around for your purpose are two different things. Only you can find your real purpose. Your transformation is waiting for you.

CHAPTER 7

# MEDITATION AND WHY IT HELPS

Empaths are always carrying around a lot of baggage in their energy fields and bodies. Meditation is an example of a method for letting those attachments dissolve and lessen. Meditation is a way to discover your truest self and give yourself permission to thrive and be your sensitive self. You won't be striving but caring for yourself and nourishing your soul. Let's look at some of the benefits of meditation.

## Meditation reduces Stress:

All humans are troubled by distracting thoughts and negative energies. For the empath, these thoughts are not your own. Meditation allows you to replace these thoughts with peace.

## Being a Reminder for Others:

You can also serve as a calm reminder for other people, showing them the level of peace that is available to them at any time.

## Building up your Prefrontal Cortex:

In addition to helping yourself and others, meditation can help you strengthen your prefrontal cortex, which is responsible for self-awareness and controlling impulses. This allows you to be more productive, more creative, and to enhance your cognition.

## Meditation Enhances your Performance Abilities:

Mediation can help you be better at sports, in business, and in personal relationships. This will calm you down so you're not distracted from performing your best.

## Better Decision-making:

When you meditate enough, you will be able to make choices from a calm, relaxed state of mind instead of a fearful and stressed out one.

## Being more present:

You can be more present when you meditate more. This will enable you to be in alignment with your truest self instead of whipped about by your circumstances.

## It can bring Enlightenment:

Keeping your ego at bay is one of the main benefits of regular meditation. This enables you true self to shine forth and the emotional baggage, criticism, and judgment can all melt away from your mind.

## Meditation can bring you Happiness:

Being truly happy with yourself is hard. This involves not choosing or needing outside stimuli. Meditation can clear your thoughts in a simple way, allowing you to just exist.

## Your own Therapy:

Meditation can be used as your personal source of therapy. Pay attention to what happens in your mind, allowing thoughts and feelings to come and go. Eventually, you will feel less attached to the thoughts.

## How to Meditate:

You are likely wondering how to meditate now. Here are the steps for doing that:

- **Find a Quiet Place:** The first and most important step to meditation is finding somewhere where you won't be disturbed. Find somewhere safe and comfortable to sit, either cross legged on the floor or leaning up against a wall. You can sit on a cushion if you want to.

- **Set your timer:** You can start by setting your timer for just five minutes per meditation session and start working your way up from there.

- **Breathe and be:** Next, close your eyes and start breathing as deeply as you can. Some may find it helpful to count their breaths, while others will find it better to just focus on their breath.

- **Stick with it:** Even when your thoughts start to wander, pull them back every time. Come back to your meditation practice every single day.

Eventually, you will start to see benefits from your meditation practice. You will feel less connected and attached to your negative thoughts and allow them to pass.

CHAPTER 8

# THE SEVEN CHAKRAS

Your chakras are swirling wheels of power and energy in your body. These energy centers correspond with centers of bundled nerves in the body. Every individual chakra (there are seven) has main organs in the physical body, along with the physical, spiritual, emotional, and psychological energies we carry with us.

The whole universe is always moving. This means that it's crucial that people keep their chakras fluid, balanced, and open all the time. Your chakras affect the connection you have with your body, your intuition, other people in your life, and the entire universe.

## Most of us are Unaware of the Chakras:

The majority of people in this society live unaware of their system of chakras. However, that doesn't mean that we are not all impacted by them. A person who lives in complete ignorance of them (either on accident or willingly) may experience suffering or pain in their life but notice that they cannot figure out why.

Learning more about the topic of chakras is one method for entering a serious path of joy and ultimate self-healing.

## Using the Metaphor of a Blocked Sink Drain:

When a sever imbalance or blockage occurs in our system, the vital life force isn't able to exist or flow. In the average, modern Western mind, it can be simpler to understand everything with a physical example.

Think about a blocked sink drain. If a lot of matter gets stick in this, the drain of the sink will back up. Then it will stagnate, leading to mold and bacteria. This process is what occurs with your energy centers and chakras, too. A sink drain is quite simple to fix though. That's because a drain is just physical. Your chakra energy system, on the other hand, is a bit harder than just a sink drain to fix.

Ensuring that your chakras stay in balance and open is more difficult, but plenty easier as soon as you commit to gaining awareness of the way they function. Your spirit, physical body, spirit, and mind are all connected at all times. In other words, your awareness of any blockage in a single area will help you become aware of what needs to be fixed in the others, as well.

## Healing Yourself with the Chakras:

When you are trying to fix your troubles with the empath path, it helps to focus on your whole being instead of just single or isolated parts. Consider the example of an individual who has recently lost their spouse to cancer, and then shortly after, develops bronchitis or another serious illness.

The trauma stays stuck inside of that individual's body and chest. Then it causes pain each time they cough or even breathe.

## A related, chain Process:

That whole process will cause their heart chakra to endure pain and suffering, as a result. As soon as someone has noticed the connection between their emotional suffering and the illness that came after, they can heal quicker.

## Holistic Healing of the Being:

This process just described can also be viewed as a method for holistically healing your physical body by noticing both the grieving and the bodily sickness involved.

## How should the Empath balance their Chakras?

Even though your body appears to be only material, it's actually a field of intelligence, transmutation, and constantly moving energy. Once you think about the included physical molecules in your body, you will start to notice the existing energy fields.

## New Technology for this:

New technology is being created right this very moment. This technology can detect this subtlety in stronger detail. It also senses the energetic vibrations involved in the process. This new technology will let us to get to newer, innovative insights about fixing our chakras and our energetic bodies.

## Discovering Vedic Knowledge:

Old, historic knowledge, like Vedic knowledge, says that the energetic matter movies through discrete channels, where groups of energy gather in our body. These centers of energy are our chakras. Each of these chakras stands for an important human need or essential requirement.

## What happens when your Chakra Centers are Open?

When all or one of your chakra centers is opened up, universal energy can flow within and throughout them. This allows our needs to get met in a more effective manner. When there is some kind of imbalance or issue happening in one of your centers, there's a stagnation of stored energy.

This makes it more difficult to meet your goals, be happy, feel fulfilled, and combat levels of stress.

## Engaging in Self-Healing:

Thankfully, there are a few different methods for fixing your chakras. These include hiring a professional a counselor. However, this isn't necessary and you can do it on your own.

## What is the Process?

This process has to do with bringing your centers of energy to life. This is done with intention and careful self-love in each of these areas. As we've discussed before, meditation is a single method for doing this. In addition, focusing on specific foods, colors, and activities can help you.

Practicing this every day will lead you to lowered levels of anxiety and stress, along with complete rejuvenation of your spirit, physical body, heart, and mind.

## What is the Benefit from this Process?

Some people may be uncertain about whether the path described is appropriate for them. If you, as an empath, want to have higher levels of energy in life, want to rid yourself of emotional pain, and also want to get fix or heal bad old habits, focusing on chakra healing is a good idea for you.

## The Benefits of Commitment to the Path:

Committing to the chakra healing path will bring you to higher clarity and a simpler time with the typical changes of your existence. In addition, it will bring nourishment to your energy levels, a supplement to the path of meditation, and increased clarity. Your intuitive, inner-intelligence is going to come alive. This higher part of you will show you the method for reaching your most advanced, highest self.

## The Chakra Centers of the Body:

Every person's seven chakras are broken up into groups. This is done depending on how they function and what they affect. For instance, the initial three chakras start at your spine's bottom and are known as the matter-related energy centers of the body.

## What does this Mean for you?

Matter-related chakras means that these energy centers are more closely related to various physical aspects of life. In this next section, we are going to go over some information on each chakra, and the remainder of the guide is going to cover the rest of the energetic centers in more detail.

## Your First Chakra Center:

This center of energy, also known as the root chakra, is in control of your basic human needs, security, instincts, and your general stability. This energy center has to do with the colon, your bladder, and the spine's first three vertebrae.

As soon as your first chakra is opened up, you are no longer controlled by anxiety or fear. Instead of that, you will feel safe in all situations, regardless of what you're going through or dealing with.

## Your Second Chakra Center:

The second chakra center relates to your sexual instincts as well as your general creativity. This center of energy exists immediately below your lower belly, or immediately over your pubic bone.

## Balancing this Center:

When you make sure that this chakra is in balance, it will let your creativity move forth and flow uninhibited. If this chakra center is blocked or out of balance, you may experience a loss of libido. In other cases, you might notice unbalanced sexual drives.

## Your Third Chakra Center:

Your third chakra exists right between your breastbone and belly. This center aids you with willpower, self-image, and personal power. Any time your third chakra is out of balance or blocked up, you are likely handling self-esteem problems and addiction issues.

## Who relates Most to these Centers of Energy?

The chakras just described are known as the "earth" chakra centers which connect us to the earthly, physical realm. Those who connect with or are involved with scientific studies often feel more connected to these centers since they handle provable matters that are physically obvious.

But in order for your entire center to be in a healthy, free balance, you must bring the other chakras into healthy alignment, too. Let's take a closer look at what these deal with.

## The Connecting Chakra Center:

Your next chakra center is your fourth chakra center. This area helps connect the spirit of human beings with physical matter. The center exists right where the heart is. This energy center exists right in the middle of the line of chakras. It connects the lower chakras with the spirit-related chakra centers.

## The Bridge of the Chakras:

The heart chakra is spirit-related, but also works as a functioning bridge. The heart bridge connects the soul with emotions and the physical body. In addition, this center is the center of spiritual connection and love.

## The Efficient and All-Encompassing Middle:

As soon as you work on the group of physical chakras, you can open up the more spiritual chakras more easily. Your heart chakra center is one of the most crucial, important centers out of all of them. This is because it connects the whole system together.

## The Chakras of the Spirit:

Next, and lastly, there are the chakras that exist inside of the spirit realm.

## Your Fifth Chakra Center:

This center exists at the throat and is your way of speaking truth, expressing yourself, and sharing ideas in a verbal and implicit way. The center also includes your mouth, jaw, tongue, and neck.

## Your Sixth Chakra Center:

This center is also called the third eye chakra. It exists immediately between the eyebrows. This center also represents your intuition. All people can intuit information but not all people can recognize the voice or listen to it. Empaths are especially skilled at this, but it could still use some work.

## Your Seventh Chakra Center:

Your seventh energy center is also known as the crown chakra. It is located right at your head's crown. The crown chakra controls your connection with your highest self. It's also responsible for the possibility of attaining enlightenment.

## More on the Chakra Centers:

The chakras are important energy bundles that are lined up throughout the body. For a long time, balancing your chakras has been considered crucial for keeping up physical and spiritual wellbeing. When you commit to learning meditation, you will bring the chakras into a healthier balance place.

## What Each Chakra is connected to:

## The Root Chakra:

The root chakra, or the lowest chakra, is responsible for how connected you are to the physical world. The chakra is connected with your survival needs, like physical health, food, safety, and shelter. You may see some issues with your stomach, digestion and also your levels of confidence levels when that center isn't balanced.

## The Sacral Chakra:

The sacral chakra is connected with your general creativity in this realm. The sacral chakra also controls your reproductive organs.

## The Solar Plexus Chakra:

This chakra center is related to your intestines, digestion, and has very important spiritual and mental benefits and effects.

## The Heart Chakra:

Your heart chakra regulates the organs around the heart and also helps your body regulate its blood pressure, heart rate, and respiration. You can form a healthy emotional relationship with a partner when your heart chakra is healthy and balanced.

## The Throat Chakra:

The throat chakra deals with your expression, including verbal and nonverbal communication. If it's not balanced, that state can lead to feelings of alienation and isolation. This being out of balance may also lead to some hormonal issues or even severe infections.

## The Third Eye Chakra:

This chakra center deals with intuition, personal insight and spirituality. In addition, it handles self-esteem at every day, normal levels. When your third eye chakra is in balance, you feel connected with the external world and the people in it. When the third eye chakra center is out of balance, you will probably feel isolated.

## The Crown Chakra:

The seventh, final chakra is at the top of your head. This chakra is related to the regulation of your whole chakra system. As soon as all of your chakras are in complete balance and have healthy energy, the crown center will connect you to the outside world. When your crown chakra is in balance, you can sense peace and the universe's one-ness.

## Noticing Blocked Chakras:

When one of your chakra centers is out of balance, you will notice this, even just subconsciously. Since you are an empath and extra intuitive, you may experience nightmares or have trouble connecting to yourself and the world.

## How can you become Aware of Blockages?

The question to ask should be, how can you notice when you have an issue with out of balance chakras so it can be healed? As mentioned before, chakras get closed or thrown off balance all the time, especially for the over-stressed and overwhelmed empath.

Any time you feel this happening to you, you are not connected to the energetic flow of the world, yourself, or the universe. This disconnection will leads you to try to fix the lack by sending energy toward the energy centers that are functioning in a healthier way.

This will lead your other chakras to close off. Others may also become overactive. Both of these situations may lead to physical, emotional, and mental disturbances and disease. To be able to fix this, meditation is absolutely needed. Once you master that, you may harmonize the energetic centers, opening them up and returning to a balanced state of being.

## Testing the Chakras:

You are likely wondering how to tell which chakra centers are blocked or out of balance. There are a few ways to test this. Let's go over some methods so may fix your body's healthy and natural state of balance.

## You can take some Online Chakra Tests:

For you to figure out what needs work, you may take a chakra test online. Along with that, just reading over some of the descriptions in this guide you're reading can be enough to help you figure out how to come into alignment.

## How can you Learn More about this?

If you feel inclined, please do some further research on what energetic blockages feel like. This will help you notice the signals of something off with your chakras or alert you to present imbalances happening.

## Recognizing Subtle Signs:

Each and every chakra center comes with its own signs, emotional, mental and physical. These signs will show that your center is either under active or over-active.

## Listening to Guided Meditations for your Chakras:

This guide you are reading will give you methods and techniques for learning to meditate on your own. However, some find that guided meditation can help at first. Especially for people who have never tried to practice meditation, using an audio recording will guide you through. This technique can be very valuable.

As soon as you are used to that and have formed a habit of it, you will be able to move on to some advanced methods for meditation. These more advanced forms involve not listening to anything but your breath.

## Chakra Meditation Steps for you to Practice:

The chakras are inside of a system of closely related parts and pieces. This means that working on each by themselves is limited compared to more holistic methods of healing.

## Get Creative with your Healing:

As an empath, you have the gift of intuitive healing not only for others but for yourself. Therefore, you should supplement the guidelines in this book with meditating on each of your chakra centers. This will help you to balance your entire system.

With more and more experience, effort, and time, you can to notice any time a chakra is blocked or off and use your meditative energy to heal these specific chakras. For you to use guided meditation, just look up some audio or a meditative video for this on YouTube. Once you found a good video, just follow along with the audio directions you are listening to.

## The Steps for Chakra Meditation:

Chakra meditation can be done by anyone who is willing to practice. Here are your rules and guidelines for getting great advantages out of this experience:

Find a Quiet and Peaceful Area: Find an undisturbed area where you will be able to get away from noise and distractions for a half hour. It's helpful if the room has colors you enjoy.

## Sit on the Ground:

The next step involves sitting down on the ground, a cushion, or a comfortable chair. You must attempt to keep your spine held straight, while at the same time not putting too much stress on yourself. Next, start to breathe deeply.

## Listen to a Guided Meditation Audio:

As soon as you are in a relaxed and calm position, listen to your guided meditation audio. You can begin with an audio that is short, such as 10 minutes and make sure you use headphones.

## Finding a Chakra Meditation:

For this to work best, ideally you should specifically listen to a chakra healing meditation. A chakra healing meditation will guide you through both visualizing the chakras on their own, then as a whole by starting at the crown or at the root, then working your attention down or up.

While you listen, try your best to think about white light or golden energy flowing amongst and throughout your chakra centers, allowing them each to open them up.

## Your Guide to Meditation for each of the Chakras:

As soon as you have done some guided sessions and had success, you will most likely start to feel a lot more sensitive to energies flowing through the body every single day. Eventually, you will start connecting your emotional states and physical feelings to specific chakras, noticing right away when something is blocked or needs to be put into balance.

## Go with what you Feel:

Around that time, you may feel the need to begin focusing on specific chakras, rather than focusing on the system itself. If this is what you feel like you should go towards, this is precisely what you must do.

CHAPTER 9

# YOUR GUIDE TO HEALING MEDITATION

For a lot of people, the idea or concept meditation is frightening at best and boring at worst. Are you one of the people who are freaked out by the idea of meditating? A lot of people think they aren't capable of sitting still or that they have no time to introduce meditation to their life. Maybe you think that it's only for Buddhists or ultra-spiritual people.

But meditation is for anyone who wishes to bring their mental states into a better form of balance. Meditation is good for all people in the world and everyone should do it, especially empaths. Before proceeding with this, let's look at some specific definitions on meditation so you can feel more comfortable with what it entails.

## Meditation Defined:

Firstly, how can we define meditation? It's the practice of training and disciplining your own mind. Although this may sound really vague, it's simple and easier than it sounds.

## Transcendental Meditation:

Most likely, the best-known and most popular practice of meditation in

America is called Transcendental Meditation. You can find more about this online.

## Kundalini Meditation:

Next, there's kundalini meditation. This uses breath work, mantras, physical motions, and even hand signs (mudras). But you don't have to be a yoga student to take part in meditation.

## What is a Mantra?

You will often hear meditation discussed in conjunction with mantras. These are phrases or words that are repeated during your meditation session. They are intended to help you focus your mind on a specific intention or just to quiet it down to silence. These can help you disconnect from chaotic emotions or disturbing thoughts.

You don't have to use mantras in meditation, but some may find them helpful. If you are curious about this method, you can look up some mantra chants on YouTube to listen to.

## An Amazing Miracle Cure:

Meditation every day can bring you health, happiness, and everlasting joy. It can improve your health, release your fears, and get better at intuition and emotional management.

## You can do this Too:

You, as an empath, must prioritize this simple activity to heighten your connection and intuition. With this simple guide, you may demystify this practice. Following these steps will allow you to make more sense of your empath gift and keep yourself from getting burned out or overwhelmed in everyday situations.

## You're Guide to the Empath's Healing Meditation:

Similar to any other skill or practice, you can get results if you want it badly enough. Sure, starting out with meditation seems hard, but that's because it's something new. Most of us were not taught how to meditate, so it's hard to get used to the idea. But thankfully, it's way easier than most people think. Starting the practice only involves a desire and willingness to improve and hone your empath abilities. To start a new way of being, you just have to want to experience a new way of living.

## Setting your Intention:

To begin your practice, you should first set your intention. Throughout your practice, every day, you can affirm this intention to yourself in your mind. You can welcome this either aloud or in your mind, welcoming the new experiences it brings. Just a simple statement such as this can provide you with the enthusiasm and energy you require to keep with the practice.

## Realize it's Easy:

It's crucial to realize that any person can learn to meditate if they have the wish to do it.

## Finding the right Mood and Environment:

You should make a specific meditation space in your house that is serene, uncluttered, and quiet. This will be just for your meditation sessions. Remember that you can eventually learn how to meditate no matter where you are.

## Meditating Anywhere:

However, when you're first starting out, a quiet place is better. Then you can work your way up to meditating in the passenger seat of a car, in the bath, or on a train.

## The Sacred Space:

A lot of teachers of meditation think that you must create a space such as this for your meditation. Even in the smallest house, you may light a candle and set up a specific pillow for your meditation.

## Don't say you don't have the Time:

Whatever you do, stop telling yourself that you don't have the time to meditate. Even if you have 30 seconds or a minute to spare, this can help you calm yourself and silence your mind in meditation.

## Start with just a Minute:

If you are still resisting this idea and insisting that it's impossible, try this. Inhale on a count of five seconds, then hold it for five, then breathe out for five, hold that for five, and so on. Set your timer for one minute and see if you can add a single minute to this each day. The second day, you will do two minutes, the third day, three minutes, and so on. Does it still seem impossible to meditate?

## Finding Peace in the Heartbeat or Pulse:

Meditation is as easy as just paying attention to the pulse. This tool is great for those new to meditation. It will improve your focus and calm even the most stressful mood.

## Sit down Cross Legged:

The first step is to sit down on the floor while crossing your legs.

## Close the Eyes:

Next, keep your eyes closed and think about the area in between the eyebrows.

## Find your Goal:

Think about your goal and put it into a mantra. Maybe this is "I am intuitive and trust myself" or "I appreciate my empath abilities".

## Repeat your Mantra:

With each pulse, repeat the mantra you have chosen.

## The Benefits of this Simple Method:

The meditation listed above is available any time you want to do it. It will help you experience immense growth in just a few minutes or a single minute. Do this every single day to calm your mind and develop your inner voice.

## Peace starts inside:

This next technique is a Kundalini style meditation that is effective, easy, and fast. This can be done anytime, anywhere.

## Press your Fingers Together:

Press your first finger against your thumb, then the next finger, then the next, until you hit every finger.

## Repeat the Following:

As you touch the first finger with your thumb, say the word "peace," then as you touch the next finger, say, "starts," then as you get to the fourth ring finger, speak the word, "with," and lastly, say "me" when you hit the last, pinkie finger.

## Breathing Deeply:

While you say the words, breathe in very deeply, going as fast or slow as you want. This can be used on the bus, at your work desk, or even while you're arguing with a loved one. You can use this technique to get through the toughest of emotional situations and to release any resentment you are holding.

## Making use of your Commute to work:

You can meditate on your way to work if you take public transportation. As soon as you get seated on the bus or train, close your eyes and repeat a mantra or do the steps listed previously. This can be done each and every day on the way to and from work. You can use guided meditations for this or just make up your own steps.

## Breathing in and Out:

While you are on your commute, inhale and exhale as you say the mantra or listen to the guided meditation. Breathing is the key to all meditations.

## Focus on Positivity:

You can think about how capable you are of your job or how grateful you are to be alive. Whatever you do, focus on something positive to empower yourself.

## Bringing Meditation Everywhere:

Meditation can be done in any place at any time, even while you cook food or stand in line at the grocery store.

## Using Activity as Meditation:

When you really enjoy something, you can use it to meditate. Time spent washing the floors or cooking can help you detach from thoughts and feel more centered.

## Walking as a Meditation:

A highly popular form of meditation is a walking meditation. Any motion, especially when it's so repetitive, can be a meditation. Walking is a great activity for this because it forces you to slow down as you think of meditation. This will ground you and calm you down. Next time you are taking your lunch break or hurrying at work, slow yourself down to make yourself meditate as you walk.

## Breathing:

Breathe deeply with each step you take, feeling your feet and grounding yourself to the floor as you walk. Form a mantra of calm and peace, repeating it in your head as you take each step.

## Doing this Regularly:

Any time you are disconnected with your empath skills, stressed out, or overwhelmed, use this to reconnect with your personal power. This can connect you to the world and ground you. You will enjoy walking more and also feel happier when you get to where you're walking to.

## Using Technology Wisely:

A lot of people think that technology causes their stress, anxiety, and disconnection. However, that's just an excuse. Technology can be used to help you center yourself and free yourself from depression or anxiety. You can download meditation apps, time your meditation sessions, or look up affirmations. Technology is what brought you to this book. Just remember to use it wisely.

## Controlling Time Spent Online:

In order to feel less stressed out, you can spend less time on the internet.

You will instantly feel calmer in your everyday life if you devote your time to more wholesome and creative activities instead of being distracted by social media.

## Alternatives to the Internet:

There are many tools that can help you control this addiction and get you back on track to inner peace. Spend time in nature, be around positive influences, or just spend some time on your own. For the empath, this mental and emotional space is very important to your overall health and wellbeing.

# CONCLUSION

Thanks again for reading *Empath: The Essential Guide to Understanding and Embracing Your Gift While Using Meditation to Empower Yourself.* It's my hope that this book showed you that your empathy is one of the most beautiful traits that exists in the world right now.

Through meditation and committing to staying conscious and aware, you can find your way back to the path you were meant for. Your empathy is here for a reason and so are you. When you fully develop your gift of empathy, nothing can disturb your inner peace because you will always be able to find it. For this to be possible, however, healthy boundaries need to be set into place.

Use the shielding techniques and centering tools given to you in this book whenever they feel necessary and eventually, you will master them.

Finally, if you enjoyed this book, please take the time to leave it a positive review on Amazon. Thank you and the best of luck to you!

Made in the USA
Columbia, SC
29 December 2020